ANGELINA
Jolie

Edgar McFay

ICON
PRESS

The Publisher: Icon Press, an imprint of Folklore Publishing
Website: www.folklorepublishing.com

Library and Archives Canada Cataloguing in Publication

McFay, Edgar, 1977–
    Angelina Jolie : angel in disguise / Edgar McFay.

(Star biographies)
Includes bibliographical references.
ISBN 1-894864-25-5

    1. Jolie, Angelina, 1975– 2. Motion picture actors and
actresses—United States—Biography. I. Title. II. Series.

PN2287.J64M36 2005   791.4302'8'092   C2005-901453-9

Project Director: Faye Boer
Project Editor: Kathy van Denderen
Production: Trina Koscielnuk
Cover Design: Valentino & Burch
Book Design: Anne & Dion

Cover Image: Courtesy of International Communications Systems

Photography credits: Every effort has been made to accurately credit the sources of photographs. Any errors or omissions should be directed to the publisher for changes in future
editions. Photographs courtesy of International Communications Systems.

We acknowledge the support of the Alberta Foundation for the Arts for our publishing
program.

PC:P6

Table of Contents

Dedication

To my family.

Acknowledgments

There are several people to thank for their help in transforming my unwieldy text into the book you now hold. For the opportunity, I'd like to extend my deepest thanks and gratitude to Faye Boer. For their support and encouragement, I would like to thank my family. For her sure editing hand, Kathy van Denderen deserves my gratitude. To the Icon Press production and design staff, I'd like to thank you all as well. This book would have been the worse without all your assistance.

Introduction

I first saw *Hackers* as a teenager; days and months later, I found myself unable to remember much about the film, save for its starlet. Despite her silly moniker, Kate "Acid Burn" Libby lingered in my memory and it had everything to do with the young actress who played her: Angelina Jolie. It may have had something to do with those looks—those world-famous looks that have captivated and entranced thousands, if not millions. The pillowy lips. The jutting cheekbones that only the daughter of Jon Voight could possess. But surely it was something else, too. I never went in for the whole pinup thing so there had to be a reason why Jolie had caught my attention. Over time, I realized what it was.

> For Jolie is not just an actress, she is a star who defies convention and embodies personal liberation.

Angelina Jolie is undeniably a good actress. Even great. But it has to do with more than that. For Jolie is not just an actress, she is a star who defies convention and embodies personal liberation. Fearlessly open and transparent, Jolie's personal life (The fascination with knives! The cutting! The obsession with blood! The family feud! Her sex life—celibate or not?) has drawn the most attention, and no matter what you think of her (Is she a freak? Is she just completely uninhibited? Should she get an agent and a publicist?), Jolie is an endlessly fascinating figure.

She rises, seemingly impervious, from the ashes of the films that have lately dominated her career. Flops such as *Beyond Borders*, *Original Sin* and *Life or Something Like It* may well have ended the careers of any number of actresses, but somehow Jolie emerges glorious, an Aphrodite rising from an oyster shell. I think, in the end, that people *do* like Angelina Jolie. Not to get all Sally Field or anything, but people like her. Or at least what they see and know of her. Hers is a refreshing presence. Her unpolished manner suggests that without the money and fame, she could be just like you or me, having the same insecurities and concerns. Although, of course, she wouldn't. Few of us possess her existential fearlessness and her zest for life, and even fewer ever allow themselves to be so open, so candid, so exposed. But those who do understand well how it can be both a blessing and a curse.

Jolie has yet to deliver her cinematic masterwork; **Girl, Interrupted** and **Gia** come close, but not close enough. Still, it likely doesn't really matter to the actress. She is determined to raise a family and is unquestionably devoted in her role as a Goodwill Ambassador for the United Nations High Commission on Refugees. It's the latter that has won Jolie legions of fans, not because she is an actress but because she is an impassioned, intelligent and tireless advocate of human rights for refugees. Who among us could devote ourselves so fully to a social cause?

In the end, this biography really isn't a biography. It's impossible to catalog someone's existence and futile to even hope that you could begin to approach some idea of who and what an individual is in a few thousand words. A life, even one as well documented as Jolie's, could never be encapsulated that easily. Instead, what follows is an account of her life and work.

chapter 1

Childhood

cting, it seems, has always been in Angelina Jolie's blood. She was born in Los Angeles on June 4, 1975. Her father, actor Jon Voight, had already seared himself into the consciousness of American filmgoers with such notable films as *Midnight Cowboy* (1969), for which he received an Oscar nomination, and *Deliverance* (1972), arguably his most memorable role. Jolie's mother, an American actress with supposed Iroquois ancestry, is Marcheline Bertrand.

Angelina Jolie Voight was the second of two children; her brother, James Haven Voight, had been born two years earlier. When she was born, her father picked her up, held Angelina in his arms and gazed into her face. She looked, according to the actor, "very, very wise, like my old best friend." Marcheline and Jon made a pledge that they would watch carefully for the signs of who Angelina was meant to be and do all they could to help her achieve her potential.

From the beginning, Angelina's parents seemed certain that their children would eventually follow them into the profession of acting, bestowing on James and Angelina the middle names, respectively, of Haven and Jolie, for use as stage names. But Jolie's path to film stardom did not always seem so clearly marked, especially when she was a young girl.

Many have scrutinized Jolie's tabloid-ready past, pathologically seeking the origins of her seeming obsession with blood, self-mutilation, knives and death and, most hungrily of all, her infamous estrangement from her father. "The press likes to use the family angle," Jolie once said in an interview with *Rolling Stone*, "because then they get to include this

JOLIE FAN FACT

As a child, Angelina had a pet snake named after actor Harry Dean Stanton and a lizard named Vladmir.

whole other aspect of my life, but they're always disappointed to hear I'm not trying to hide anything about some huge, sordid estrangement between us."

The relationship between Jolie and her father is undoubtedly fractious (no doubt exasperated by the frankness with which Jolie speaks), but for the most part, Jolie has spoken fondly and openly about their past. "I never remember a time when I needed my father and he wasn't there," she said. "But he was an artist, and it was the '70s—a strange time for everybody. To this day, I think my parents really loved each other."

Despite their affection, however, Jolie's parents separated when she was just a year old. Rumor had it that Bertrand simply could no longer tolerate her husband's alleged philandering. For a while, Angelina, her brother and mother continued to live in Los Angeles, but when she was eight, they moved east to Sneden's Landing, an hour away from Manhattan. From that point, Angelina's existence became somewhat nomadic. "We always moved," she said, "I lived in a lot of different apartments. No one ever owned anything so I was never rooted anywhere."

This rootless existence may have proved stressful and traumatizing for some, but Jolie recalls that her early years were filled with happiness. On the surface, there was little to distinguish her from other young girls her age. In kindergarten, she became a part of a sorority of sorts called the Kissy Girls. "We would chase the boys around and kiss them a lot, and they would scream," she recalled to *Rolling Stone* in 2001, "and I played dress-up—I used to wear costumes all the time. I used to love those plastic high heels." For her fifth birthday party, Angelina curled her hair and applied some lipstick. "It was very girly," she described. At home, dressed up in her mother's handmade costumes, Angelina would perform with giddy delight in front of her brother's camera as he happily chortled, "Come on, Angie, give us a show!"

When there was time, Angelina accompanied her mother and brother to the theater or to Renaissance Fairs. She found the excursions endlessly fascinating, and the family attended many of them, not for the jousts or the romance of a more chivalrous age, but because Angelina loved the weapons. "I went to the Renaissance Fair when I was a little girl," she remembered, "and there were all these knives. There's something really beautiful and traditional about them. Different countries have different weapons and blades, and there's something beautiful about them to me. So I began collecting knives. I've collected weapons since I was a little girl." Knives certainly aren't what girls, or boys for that matter, usually amass, but by then Angelina was starting to feel just a little different from everyone else. While all the other little girls "wanted to be a ballerina, [she] kind of wanted to be a vampire."

When Angelina was nine, her maternal grandfather passed away. The funeral proved riveting, touching something deep within her soul. She loved how a funeral allowed individuals to reach out and connect with one another and how it was a ritual invested with centuries of tradition and significance. For the little girl who had never known a steady home, there was something comforting about the funeral, and Angelina began harboring dreams of becoming a funeral director. "I'm very drawn to some things that are tradition and that are roots. I think that may be why I focused on funerals." The happiness of her early childhood was beginning to recede and, in its place, a disconsolation and depression began to settle in. Out went the plastic high heels and shimmering sparkles; in came the red and black leather, dog collars and studs.

Angelina and her family moved back to Los Angeles when she

"I went to the Renaissance Fair when I was a little girl," she remembered, "and there were all these knives. There's something really beautiful and traditional about them."

was eleven. The move did little to alleviate the despair growing inside her. Although she insists that there wasn't a single event that catalyzed her depression, Jolie recalled that when she was ten, life "started not to be fun." Her earliest childhood memory is of lying in her crib, looking out towards the sky from the window. The image becomes a metaphor. "I've just been staring out a window all my life," she said, "thinking there was somewhere I could finally be grounded and happy. I belonged somewhere else." Although her name means "sweet little angel," she hardly felt like one.

Whatever the cause of these feelings, the effect upon Angelina was all too concrete and real. When she had first returned to Los Angeles, Angelina had enrolled at the respected Lee Strasberg Theatre Institute. Lee Strasberg, best known for his role as the duplicitous Hyman Roth in *The Godfather Part II* and for his promotion of method acting, opened the school in 1969, following a beloved and lauded career at the Actors Studio in New York City. It was there that he taught and mentored acting luminaries such as Paul Newman, Al Pacino, Jack Nicholson and Robert de Niro.

Method acting has been stereotyped and lampooned to negative effect, but as a whole, its impact has been nothing less than explosive and revolutionary. It requires creative expression, a need to explore the abstractions of acting and submersion within the mind and soul of another individual. It's a challenging and draining technique, demanding that actors delve into their past to find the emotions necessary to perform.

Jolie's early tutelage would become patently clear in the roles that have thus far defined her career—as the doomed supermodel Gia Carangi in the HBO film, *Gia*, and as the volatile Lisa

Rowe in *Girl, Interrupted.* In both films, Jolie disappeared fully into the characters, with whom she had, unfortunately, much in common. But for now, she was a young, confused child who left the Lee Strasberg Theatre Institute after two years, claiming that she "didn't have the memories" so crucial to method acting, and this signaled her hasty, but ultimately short-lived, retreat from the profession.

At school, Angelina hated that she had to sit still, so while her teachers rambled on about math or history, she sat at her desk and covered the pages of her notebooks with drawings. Images of swords, daggers and other stabbing implements filled her books. Words accompanied some of her sketches; dire sentiments such as "DEATH: EXTINCTION OF LIFE" and "AUTOPSY: EXAMINATION OF A CORPSE" and, quite simply, "SUICIDE." The first two sentiments reflected Jolie's desire to become a funeral director. The last, of course, needs no explanation. "Thirteen, fourteen—that was a bad time," Jolie said simply. "Yeah. Very."

At the tender age of 13, Angelina began contemplating suicide. Or as she puts it, she began thinking about "not wanting to be around anymore." It had all become so difficult and, suddenly, it seemed easier just to say goodbye to it all than to keep going. She felt too much like an outsider. She was teased mercilessly by classmates at Beverly Hills High for her braces and glasses and for her gangly body that had yet to develop. Her penchant for wearing black and dying her hair only served as more fodder for her classmates.

And even though her father was an actor, Angelina hardly lived a life of celebrity. Her family had enough money, but it certainly wasn't in the amounts of her far more fortunate classmates. While they shopped on Rodeo Drive, Jolie scoured the bins of Los Angeles thrift

...while her teachers rambled on about math or history, she sat at her desk and covered the pages of her notebooks with drawings.

shops. Angelina protested to her teacher one day that she couldn't type her papers on a computer because she didn't have one, and the teacher simply said, "Have your father buy you one." When she attempted to model, as many of her classmates did, it was a failure. "I was too short, too scarred, too fat, too everything else," she said. Scarred. Oh yes, the scars.

Along the jaw line of Jolie's face, just below those pillowy bee-stung lips, is the faintest trace of a scar. She's had it since she was 14, a mark left by her first serious boyfriend, a punk who must have seemed a world away from the manicured hallways of Beverly Hills High and its roving bands of cliques. The boyfriend lived with Angelina's family for two years, and he and Angelina began experimenting with S&M and the knives for which she had become infamous. She carved an X into her arm, slashed at her stomach and cut her neck, an act that nearly killed her. "I went to hospital," she said in an interview with *Woman's Day* in 2000, "I nearly cut my jugular vein."

"Looking back," she said of the relationship, "he was somebody that I wanted to help me break out and I would get frustrated when he couldn't help me. Which was when the knives came in—he'd be asked to cut me or I'd cut him." One naturally wonders why she would do this. Psychologists point out that out of 100,000 people, between 700 and 750 self-mutilate and that it is highly prevalent among single, Caucasian females in their teens or early 20s. The pain they inflict upon themselves is seen as a relief from psychological stress and crisis.

However, Jolie's explanation is far more blunt and succinct. Numbed and detached, she cut herself just to feel something human and tactile. "I was trying to feel something," she said in a 1999 interview with *Access Hollywood*, "I was looking at different things. It felt so primitive and it felt so honest, but then I had to deal with not telling my mother, hiding things, wearing gauze bandages to school."

> The relationship with her boyfriend ended when Angelina was 16. "It was a tough breakup," she said. "That relationship felt like a marriage." Angelina, disillusioned, swore off dating.

The darkness that enveloped her during this period of her life seemed to be behind her. It would return to haunt her, but for the time being, Angelina was confident and able to put her demons to rest. "By the time I was 16," she said, "I had gotten it all out of my system," referring to the self-mutilation, which she emphatically does not condone.

With a newfound sense of purpose, Angelina threw herself into acting. Seeking independence, she finished school at 16 and moved into an apartment a few blocks away from her mother's home. The minute she began to take the craft seriously, everyone around her realized the breadth and depth of her talents. In just a few short years, Angelina, the vampire-loving, gawky outcast of Beverly Hills High, would begin her meteoric ascent into the pantheon of Hollywood stars.

15

chapter 2

Alone in New York

Angelina's first film appearance was in 1982 when she was seven years old, with the release of Hal Ashby's *Lookin' to Get Out.* Her father was the star and co-writer of the film, which helped her to get the part. In the film, Angelina played a role that couldn't have been much of a stretch for her. She was Tosh, the young estranged daughter of itinerant gambler Alex Kovac, played by Jon Voight. The film was a family affair, with mother Marcheline Bertrand credited as "Girl in Jeep." The film wasn't exactly a runaway success, financially or critically, and Angelina's role was relatively minor, but

The modeling agents who had once dismissed her for being too fat or too short now clamored for her exotic and undeniable beauty.

through it, young Angelina discovered the acting world. Combined with her frequent childhood trips to the theater, the experience must surely have bred in Angelina a love for the craft.

She had her stage debut at the age of 15 at the Lee Strasberg Theatre Institute in a role that had originally been written for a man, but Angelina found something appealing about "the big, fat forty-year-old German man." Already, the budding actress was demonstrating a wonderfully refreshing eclectic taste that would become her hallmark. Mr. Wagner, or Frau Wagner as Angelina played him, was a dominatrix. Jolie's father, who was in the audience, was "a little shocked," but the shock came from the realization that, 'Oh my God, she's just like me.'" Her performance only reinforced what Voight had long believed: his daughter had the nascent talent to be a great actress. "From the beginning," he said, "there were signals along the way," referring fondly

to the young Angelina's penchant for dressing up in costume and her undeniable presence. Still, at 15, Angelina wasn't entirely convinced of a future in acting.

Her looks, once the object of scorn, were now much in demand. The modeling agents who had once dismissed her for being too fat or too short now clamored for her exotic and undeniable beauty. Jolie signed with the Finesse Modeling Agency and embarked on a modeling career, appearing in photo spreads from London to New York, and in the occasional music video, notably Meat Loaf's *Rock 'n' Roll Dreams Come Through* and clips for both The Lemonheads and Lenny Kravitz.

This work brought her financial stability, and by the time she was 19, Jolie was able to afford her own apartment in Los Angeles. For the first time in her life, Jolie was living in a home that wasn't rented or leased. She also took her first tentative steps towards movie stardom. Dropping her famous last name, Angelina Jolie Voight became, simply, Angelina Jolie. Although much has been made of the name change, Jolie reveals that she did so only because she felt it "important to be [her] own person."

In 1993, the film *Cyborg 2: Glass Shadow* premiered, and Jolie played the role of the cyborg, Casella "Cash" Reese. The film wasn't exactly a blockbuster, and it wasn't a critical favorite either. Directed by Michael Schroeder (whose previous credits included the similarly obscure and forgotten films *Dead On: Relentless II* and *Damned River*), *Cyborg 2: Glass Shadow* had been conceived as a sequel to the 1989 original, *Cyborg*. In 1989,

Cyborg, starring the then relatively unknown Jean-Claude van Damme, surprised many box office watchers when it managed to gross over $10 million on a budget of an estimated $2 million, and it also launched the American moviegoer's brief love affair with the "Muscles from Brussels."

Cyborg 2: Glass Shadow was received so poorly that it was given the filmic kiss of death—it went straight to video. Perhaps it was the absence of Jean-Claude van Damme, seen that year in the films *Hard Target* and *Nowhere to Run*, or perhaps it was that few people, even *Cyborg* fans, were clamoring for a sequel. However, *Cyborg 2: Glass Shadow* does mark Jolie's return to film, though it was probably more memorable for her bared breasts.

Jolie's character in the film, Casella "Cash" Reese, is caught between two international conglomerates, Pinwheel Robotics and Kobayashi. Both corporate giants manufacture the cyborgs, without which 21st-century society would be absolutely helpless. Eager to increase its profit margin, Kobayashi begins programming its cyborgs to become assassins, methodically and effectively ridding itself of its competition. Obviously unhappy with the turn of events, Martin Dunn, head of Pinwheel Robotics, reacts by creating the gorgeous but deadly Casella to be the ultimate suicide bomber. He injects her with a liquid explosive named, of course, Glass Shadow, which ignites in the event that Casella has an orgasm. Or something like that.

As it is with most cyborg movies made ever since the release of *Blade Runner*, Casella is blessed with emotion and independent thought. Once she experiences the power of love in the arms of her martial arts instructor, Colson Ricks (also known as Colt .45), assassinating the CEO of Kobayashi suddenly becomes a low priority. She just wants to love and to live. With the help of a sympathetic cyborg mercenary

> **Cyborg 2: Glass Shadow** was received so poorly that it was given the filmic kiss of death—it went straight to video.

subtly named Mercy, played inexplicably by a slumming Jack Palance, Casella and Colson flee for the paradise of Mombasa, where unlicensed cyborgs can live freely. Giving chase is a corporate bounty hunter, Danny Bench (one supposes that Danny Robothunter would have been too obvious), played by Billy Drago. Drago, who was so menacingly effective as Frank Nitti in *The Untouchables*, is merely pitiful here as a drug-addled cyborg tracker. Martial arts high jinks and flashbacks to the first film ensue before the film reaches its conclusion.

There is little salvageable about the film, and with its nonsensical and convenient plot (Palance's Mercy chooses as his hideout a ship that he once commanded; Casella escapes from Pinwheel by throwing a gun at a security officer who, while falling backwards, pulls its trigger and mows down the pursuing guards), audiences reacted in kind. *Cyborg 2: Glass Shadow* was quickly forgotten.

Whatever currency and relevancy *Cyborg* had bought with audiences had been spent, and the film failed to capitalize on the phenomenal success of another cyborg film, *Terminator 2: Judgment Day*, released two years earlier. The failure of *Cyborg 2: Glass Shadow* and its dismal reception precipitated a return of the depression that had haunted Jolie as a child.

"I didn't know if I wanted to live because I just didn't know what I was living for," the actress said in a 2001 interview with **Rolling Stone**. Alone in a New York City hotel room, Jolie laid out plans to take her own life. It would, of course, involve her passion—knives—and an overdose of sleeping pills. She wrote a note to the housekeeper, asking her to call the police and thus be spared the gruesome task of discovering Jolie's corpse. Jolie spent the remaining day walking the streets. She stopped at one store and almost bought a kimono but then realized the impracticality of such a purchase when you don't plan on being around to wear it.

She returned to her hotel room and realized that she might not have the stomach to slash her own wrists. It would have to be the sleeping pills. But as Jolie looked over the pills, she thought of the horrible burden of guilt her suicide would place on her mother, who had previously sent Jolie some pills when she had needed some. And, as she sat alone in her room, she arrived at an epiphany. "We can make that decision anytime," she later told *Rolling Stone*, "and I kind of lay there with myself and thought, 'You might as well live a lot, really hard and not give a sh**, because you can always walk through that door.' So I started to live as if I could die any day."

With a renewed sense of purpose, and perhaps to symbolize this promise to herself, she returned to the store and bought the kimono the very next day. Fate, it seemed, had other plans for Jolie, plans far more glorious and fulfilling than an ignoble death.

Her next film, *Hackers*, was far from being a critical or popular success, but the film did bring her positive reviews for her performance and, perhaps more importantly, love.

introducing
Jonny

One would be hard pressed to remember Hollywood's cyber-mania in 1995. Despite their relevancy and big name casts, the films during this year (Ralph Fiennes' *Strange Days*, Sandra Bullock's *The Net*, Keanu Reeves' *Johnny Mnemonic* and Denzel Washington's and Russell Crowe's *Virtuosity*) failed to capture with any sort of precision or immediacy the cybernetic world that had been so brilliantly imagined and conceived in the books of William Gibson, notably *Neuromancer*. The films were overlooked in favor of the talking pig, *Babe*, the decidedly low-tech romance of *The Bridges of Madison County*, and the murk and grit of *The Usual Suspects* and *Se7en*.

Despite filmmakers' best efforts, the cybernetic films failed to overcome the inherent tedium of their plots: people sitting at computer terminals just aren't all that exciting. The films certainly did foreshadow the stunning visuals and mind-bending twists that would embody the best of *The Matrix* (1999), but for the most part, they had little impact. The same could also be said of Jolie's next film, *Hackers* (1995).

Shortly after the release of *Cyborg 2: Glass Shadow*, Jolie landed a role in *Hackers*, which was MGM's entry in Hollywood's cyber-sweepstakes. The film was definitely made with youth in mind. Its cast was composed of young and attractive up-and-comers who roller-blade their way through the canyons of New York City to a techno-heavy soundtrack featuring the then fashionable musical group The Prodigy. Among the cast were Jesse Bradford, who would go on to find success in the cheer fest *Bring it On*, and teen movie staple, Matthew Lillard, who would later star in Wes Craven's *Scream*, Robert Iscove's *She's All That* and play a pitch-perfect Shaggy in the *Scooby-Doo* franchise.

The star of *Hackers* was the dashing British actor Jonny Lee Miller, who would earn much more notice a year later in the groundbreaking and controversial film *Trainspotting*, as Sick Boy. *Hackers'* director was Iain Softley, who had garnered acclaim and notice with *Backbeat* (1994), a resonant exploration of The Beatles early days.

Hackers was released on September 15, 1995. The two high-tech thrillers that preceded it, **The Net** and **Virtuosity**, had failed to surpass or even meet expectations, ominous signs to be sure. But still, with its photogenic cast and credible director, there were hopes that **Hackers** would avoid the fate of its predecessors. It was not to be.

Although some critics found the film enjoyable—Roger Ebert deemed the film "well directed, written and acted…smart and entertaining"—other reviews were not so positive. Hal Hinson of *The Washington Post* was far from diplomatic when he called the film "super-superficial, cacophonous and dumb." Other critics found *Hackers* visually appealing but tedious and hopelessly bogged down beneath the weight of its own technical gobbledygook and its rather banal plot. It didn't help, of course, that its villains, Fisher Stevens and a pre-*Sopranos* Lorraine Bracco, were little more than cartoons.

In the film, Dade Murphy (a smugly self-assured Jonny Lee Miller) returns to the world of hacking computers seven years after nearly engineering a major stock market crash while he wormed his way into the networks of top Wall Street investment and banking firms. Upon his return to New York City, Dade meets up with a group of hackers who draw him back into the art. Among them is Jolie's Kate Libby, or as she is more commonly known by her hacker nom de plume, Acid Burn. When Dade meets Kate, their relationship is predictably caustic as the two sullen souls dance around and towards each other.

In the meantime, they hack, and in their travels along the Information Superhighway, they encounter a former hacker named The Plague (Fisher Stevens), who now uses his considerable talents to sniff out hackers and to siphon funds from corporate bank accounts for himself and his mistress (Lorraine Bracco). The Plague's work has not gone unnoticed, but savvy operator that he is, he's constructed a trail that leads not to him, but to Dade and his motley crew. And to ensure his freedom, The Plague has created a computer virus that could destroy five supertankers within minutes.

Despite the film's tediousness, Jolie's performance lingers in the memory. She exudes a certain sexuality, arrogance and willfulness that, at times, proves remarkably buoyant. With her hair shorn in a pixie cut, Jolie's exotic looks—her pouty lips, angular cheeks and dark and soulful eyes—are prominently on display. To her credit, she is able to convey a sweet vulnerability and humanity to what easily could have been a one-dimensional role. When she and Jonny Lee Miller interact, their chemistry is palpable and engaging. They bring a vivacity that is sorely lacking in much of the film.

Hackers brought Jolie some of the best reviews of her nascent career. And it's no surprise that Jolie and Miller shared an obvious and luminous synergy. Life often mirrors art, and just as Dade and Kate fall in love, so too did Angelina and Jonny. Jolie and Miller met on set, and though they did their best to keep their relationship a secret, it was difficult for them to contain their happiness. Jolie spoke often of how they shared an apartment during the film's shoot, and Miller spoke of being involved with an American girl from Los Angeles.

> She exudes a certain sexuality, arrogance and willfulness that, at times, proves remarkably buoyant.

Jonny Lee Miller was born in Kingston, England, on November 15, 1972. His father was a stage manager, and his mother was involved in production. His grandfather was Bernard Lee, who played the character "M" in the James Bond films. It was, ironically, Miller's portrayal of the James Bond–Sean Connery obsessed Sick Boy in

Hackers (1995)

Trainspotting that proved to be his big acting break. Interested in theater from an early age, Miller made his television debut at the age of 11 in the miniseries *Mansfield Park*. He made appearances in such respected series as *Inspector Morse* and the critically acclaimed *Prime Suspect* franchise. In the latter, Miller admirably held his own against the supremely sublime Helen Mirren. *Hackers* marked the Englishman's film debut.

Before filming on *Hackers* even began, the actors were required to delve deeply into research. Just as parts of the film's jargon-heavy script confused audiences, so too did it puzzle the actors. "With a lot of lines," Jolie confessed to *Empire Magazine* in 1996, "I didn't know what I was talking about, but it was fascinating."

To become familiar with the subject, the actors read books on computers and met with computer hackers. To prepare for the film's climax, which involved racing through the streets of New York and the cavernous halls of Grand Central Station on roller blades and hacking The Plague's computer network, the actors spent three weeks in classes learning how to roller blade and how to type. The research also helped the cast to connect and to bond with one another. "Hanging out with the cast…was heaven," Jolie revealed to *Empire Magazine*. "Racing Jonny on roller blades was a big part of our relationship."

To casual observers, the relationship seemed odd. Miller was definitely charming, though shy and soft-spoken. Jolie, on the other hand, was brash and loud, with a ballyhooed wild streak. But perhaps he was the yin to her yang, and the couple was undeniably happy. Miller, acknowledging the media's perception of his partner, said in an interview, "Jolie's image is of a wild, crazy, femme fatale. But she's not. She's a very nice big-hearted girl." For Jolie, Miller was the first man she had met in a very long time whom she felt was worth her time and commitment. "I had my first boyfriend when I was 14," Jolie told *B Magazine*, "and then I didn't sleep with anybody until I met [Jonny] at 19."

The pair married in May 1996, but before their union Jolie had a brief, but much celebrated, relationship with Jenny Shimizu, a Calvin Klein model-turned-actress, which marked the press' fascination with Jolie's candid bisexuality. In an interview with *Elle* in 2000, Jolie, speaking with the frankness that has made her

such a riveting figure, said, "Honestly, I like everything. Boyish girls, girlish boys, the heavy and the skinny. Which is a problem when I'm walking down the street."

She first met Shimizu while filming *Foxfire,* and from the start, Jolie was in love. "I realized that I was looking at her in a way that I had looked at men," she said in an interview with *Rolling Stone.* "And it was great, and it was a discovery. It had never crossed my mind that I was going to one day experiment with or kiss a woman; it was never something I was looking for. I just happened to fall for a girl." The affair was brief (Shimizu went on to date Ione Skye of *Say Anything*) and Jolie, who had stayed in close contact with Miller, returned to her Englishman, though she later admitted that if she hadn't married him, she might very well have married Shimizu.

At the wedding, Jolie wore black leather pants and a white blouse with Jonny's name emblazoned on it, in her own blood. "We didn't have a big white wedding," Jolie said wryly to *Empire Magazine* in 1996, "we had a small black wedding." Love was certainly a factor in their union, though many have speculated that after a childhood of uncertainty and confusion, Jolie was seeking some semblance of stability in her life. Of course, getting married may have been something as simple as an impulse. "I always fall in love while I'm working on a film," she said. "It's such an intense thing. And I've always been at my most impulsive when English men are around. They get to me."

chapter 4

More than a Bionic Babe

lthough *Hackers* was a less than a spectacular success, Jolie dismissed its failure casually. "It taught me a good lesson," she said. "A lot of young actors take themselves so seriously that unless we're crying and screaming we don't think we're acting. There's something to just being present, being in the moment and having a good time." Jolie certainly had her fun, and the energy with which she had tackled the role of Kate Libby caught Hollywood's attention. The offers began pouring in.

But, with the fierce independence and eclecticism for which Jolie has become famous (or infamous), she refused many of the offers, certainly a bold move at a time when her career was just beginning to bloom in an exceptionally fickle industry. The majority of the roles offered to Jolie during this time were obviously given with her past performances in mind, namely *Cyborg 2: Glass Shadow* and *Hackers*. "I seem to be getting a lot of things pushed my way that are strong women," she said in an interview in 1996, "but the wrong type of strong women. It's like people see *Hackers* and they send me offers to play tough women with guns, the kind who wear no bra and a little tank top. I'd like to play strong women who are also very feminine." (This is a rather ironic comment, considering that Jolie would later have her greatest commercial success playing the ultimate in tough women with guns and tank tops as Lara Croft of the *Tomb Raider* franchise.)

It's clear that Jolie was trying to avoid the sort of typecasting that can turn an actor into a cliché and a punch line. "I usually try to look for something I haven't

"I usually try to look for something I haven't done before, a side of me that I haven't completely explored."

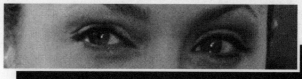

done before, a side of me that I haven't completely explored," she said in a 1998 interview with Box Office Online. "There's a truth in acting, and there is a very real part of me that can understand that or can believe in that or can see the beauty of that or see the ugliness in that and the statement that needs to be made."

In 1996, she followed *Hackers* with roles in three films: the romantic comedy *Love Is All There Is*, the dark, romantic adventure *Mojave Moon* and the drama *Foxfire*. *Love Is All There Is*, an update of Shakespeare's Romeo and Juliet, had actually been filmed in 1994 but was only given a theatrical release in the fall of 1996. Interestingly enough, the film's opening credits claim to "introduce" Jolie, who had, of course, already appeared in two films.

Love Is All There Is failed to find an audience, even though reviews were generally favorable. Lawrence Van Gelder of the *New York Times* called it a "buoyant, wickedly funny comedy," while the *Chicago Sun-Times* lauded the actors' "fine double-takes, posturing and body language." The cast boasted Lainie Kazan (who would reprise a similar role in the smash *My Big Fat Greek Wedding*), Paul Sorvino (worlds removed from *Goodfellas*), Barbara Carrera (a Bond girl from *Never Say Never Again*) and Dick Van Patten (the harried father of the popular television sitcom *Eight is Enough*).

The plot, a happy convergence of serendipity and fate, revolves around the simmering rivalry between the humble, working-class Cappamezzas and the snotty, pretentious Malacicis. The Cappamezzas own a small, struggling, family-run Sicilian restaurant, apparently doomed to bankruptcy with the opening of the elegant and upscale Florentine Malacicis' eatery. Matters are further complicated when Rosario Cappamezza (Nathaniel

Marston—currently in the soap opera *One Life to Live*) is cast as Romeo in a student production of Romeo and Juliet, and the original Juliet (a particularly hefty girl) causes the balcony to collapse. Brought in as her replacement is Jolie's Gina Malacici.

Although few would mistake Jolie for a native Italian with her sometimes-flimsy Italian accent, the role did present a dimension to the actress not seen in the high-tech thrillers that signaled her return to acting. Unfortunately, not many people saw the film when it was in theaters, though it has, admittedly, found an audience on late-night television and with fans of Jolie. *Love Is All There Is* was recently released on DVD, and Jolie's face is prominently displayed on its cover, an obvious attempt to capitalize on the rising fame of its then obscure Juliet.

Mojave Moon was another foray into romantic comedy for Jolie, but it had a darker edge far removed from the farce and broad laughs of *Love Is All There Is*. *Mojave Moon* boasted a solid cast, with Danny Aiello (brilliantly understated in Spike Lee's *Do the Right Thing*), Anne Archer (underused in both *Patriot Games* and *Clear and Present Danger*), Alfred Molina (Doc Ock in *Spider-Man 2*) and Michael Biehn (1980s film staple of *Navy SEALs*, *The Terminator*, *The Abyss* and *Aliens*). Unfortunately, the film's convoluted and self-consciously "offbeat" plot wanders through the Mojave Desert towards its jarring conclusion. Its director, Kevin Dowling, would go on to find better work as a television director, working on such programs as the wonderfully offbeat dramedies *Ed*, *Gilmore Girls* and the sturdy *Judging Amy*.

The plot of *Mojave Moon*, such as it is, involves the middle-aged, newly divorced car salesman Al McCord (Aiello), a recent Los Angeles transplant hoping for a new beginning. Stopping in for a bite at a diner, he catches the eye of oversexed jailbait Eleanor "Ellie" Rigby (Jolie), who wastes no time in telling Al that she was indeed named after The Beatles' song. When Ellie asks Al to drive her back to the trailer park home that she shares with her mother in the Mojave Desert, Al, ever lustful, agrees. When he arrives at the trailer park, Al encounters Ellie's mother, the

bizarre but sweet Julie (Archer) and Ellie's clearly psychotic, unstable boyfriend, Boyd (Biehn). The moon is full and surreally large, so, naturally, there must be something weird and magical in the air. Al and Julie dance beneath the moonlight and eventually fall asleep. And so begins an odd series of unfortunate events that include the discovery of Boyd's seemingly dead body in Al's trunk, Al's stolen wallet, a car that won't start and, finally, a messy love triangle (both Ellie and Julie fall for the ordinary Al while Boyd seethes with rage) that resolves itself ever so neatly atop a cliff.

Reviews of *Mojave Moon* ranged from favorable to scathing, but many agreed that Jolie, as the mercurial Ellie, made the most of her role. Some reviewers, as always, were careful to note Jolie's fleeting scenes of nudity. Freudians, of course, have returned to this film, pointing out that the May-December romance between Ellie and Al was a foreshadow of Jolie's eventual marriage to Billy Bob Thornton. However, *Mojave Moon* was just another movie, and it was another relative failure of Jolie's young and fragile career.

Jolie's next film, *Foxfire*, released in August 1996, was an adaptation of the book by Joyce Carol Oates. Female empowerment is the theme as four high-school students, who have all been sexually harassed at the hands of their biology teacher, are inspired to fight back when a mysterious drifter walks in one day from the rain and into their timid and sedated lives. Cast as the drifter "Legs" Sadovsky, Jolie once again admirably married her inherent sensuality to a flinty sensibility. It was a role, in character, similar to that of Kate Libby in *Hackers*, but that's where the similarity ends. While Kate was little more than a two-dimensional foil, Legs Sadovsky is front and center, the soul and emotional core of *Foxfire*. In her first starring role, Jolie was praised for her "beguiling portrayal," but the film, for the most part,

It was during the filming of *Foxfire* that Jolie became intimately acquainted with the actress Jenny Shimizu, who played the pothead Goldie.

resonated little with audiences and had the misfortune of opening just days after *Girls Town*, a movie with similar themes and plot elements.

Legs' gang consisted of characters who were given little depth and who were little more than archetypes: Maddy, the narrator, is the girl next door; Rita is the true-blue virgin, while Violet is promiscuous; and Goldie is the requisite stoner. Although the film has moments of genuine depth and insight, they are few and far between. Instead, the movie quickly unravels when the girls are expelled from school after leaving their biology teacher bloodied and battered. They hole themselves up in an abandoned house on the outskirts of town and engage in some free-spirited rebellion that includes theft, car-jacking and kidnapping.

The film's message of female empowerment, though noble, is somewhat undercut in a lingering tattooing scene during which Legs brands her gang's breasts, and by the Sapphic overtones of the relationship between Legs and Maddy that are never fully or truly explored but are exploited for titillation instead.

The film is better remembered these days not for its artistic or thematic merits but for the true-life events that might have been culled from the script itself. It was during the filming of *Foxfire* that Jolie became intimately acquainted with the actress Jenny Shimizu, who played the pothead Goldie.

The failures of these three early films could very well have doomed Jolie's career. Hollywood rewards success but turns its back with whiplash-inducing speed on actors whose films fail to reap financial windfalls. Studio corridors are littered with promising actors and actresses whose stars waned with box office failures, their careers transformed into trivia answers and cautionary tales. One need only look to the filmographies of once rising actors such as *Fast Times at Ridgemont High*'s Phoebe Cates, *The Breakfast Club*'s Molly Ringwald and *St. Elmo's Fire*'s Rob Lowe to see just how quickly and perilously a career can slide into obscurity. Jolie, however, would retreat wisely from film and find work in the creatively liberated world of cable television and would prove her abilities.

chapter 5

farewell Jonny.
Hello Gia.

As happy as Jolie and Miller might have appeared just weeks after their marriage, their union, though never fractious, ultimately withered, giving great tongue-clicking satisfaction to observers who'd always claimed that it was an ill-fated match. Their marriage, for all intents and purposes, was over after only a few months. It was something neither of them could have predicted, but as happens all too often, the reality of marriage was far from the ideal. Pressures from their careers and the restlessness of youth conspired to place too much strain upon the marriage.

"We were simply too young," Jolie admitted. "I was so lucky to have met the most amazing man, who I wanted to marry. It comes down to timing." And the timing was poor. Jolie was working steadily, plunging deep into the roles that would

ultimately be her breakthroughs. Although she was in love, Jolie was unwilling to become a wife, choosing instead to devote her time and energy to her career.

In an interview with the *Calgary Sun*'s Louis Hobson, Jolie said that she wasn't "present enough, physically or emotionally, in relationships to get serious. It's not fair to the other person that I'm so busy with my career and that I'm often distant even when I am with someone." Jolie once told her husband while filming the 1998 HBO biopic *Gia*, a role that would vault her to stardom, that he wouldn't see or speak to her for weeks, so deeply did she immerse herself in the role: "I'm alone, I'm dying, I'm gay. I'm not going to see you for weeks." The fissure existing between them precluded any sort of emotional and spiritual intimacy, leaving their marriage just a husk. Jolie lamented, "I

wanted more for him than I could give. He deserves more than I am prepared to give at this time in my life."

Restlessness played a part in the breakup of their marriage too. Miller wanted to leave the United States and return to England, while Jolie was firm in her desire to remain in New York and go to film school. It's clear that the separation was devastating, and it seems that it was something neither of them truly wanted, but in the end, the reality of their circumstances trumped their own desires. Jolie and Miller postponed the signing of their divorce papers for years following the separation but eventually chose, unhappily, to make the divorce official in 1999. The two remain close, and Jolie later admitted that divorcing Miller was one of the dumbest things that she had done.

For the moment, however, the dissolution of their marriage marked the return of the darkness and angst that had first plagued Jolie when she was a teenager. Poetically, these dark days preceded Jolie's earliest successes as an actress in the television films *George Wallace* and *Gia*.

Jolie's role in *Gia* proved to be especially taxing for her, which is understandable given the weighty and demanding subject matter. More than 200 actresses auditioned for the lead role, yet none seemed to possess the necessary depth. Producers needed a young actress capable of blending femininity with toughness, of transcending reality and yet, at the same time, being firmly rooted within it. Jolie, relatively unknown at the time, was cast for the role. Her resemblance to the doomed supermodel, both physically and spiritually, was eerie. Director Michael Cristofer, in an

Gia (1998)

interview with *Entertainment Weekly*, explained that "Jolie [was] probably as adventurous a person as Gia in many ways…she has the quality which I am told Gia had—a pervasive innocence and vulnerability, which I thought was a quality desperately needed. In the hands of the wrong actress, I think Gia could be a person you didn't really want to be in the same room with."

Gia Marie Carangi's life story reads like a fairy tale gone bad. Born in a working-class section of Philadelphia on January 29, 1960, Gia had a troubled childhood marked by her parents' divorce and by a rootless existence as she was shuttled between two households. As a child, she possessed a rebellious streak, often breaking curfews and experimenting with alcohol, pills and drugs. It was permanence and stability that Gia sought, and she found it in the gay clubs of downtown Philadelphia, where the relaxed attitudes towards all types of sexuality provided comfort and release for her own leanings.

At 17, while at the club DCA, Gia, who had by this time developed the exotic looks and curvaceous figure for which she became famous, caught the eye of hairstylist and aspiring photographer, Maurice Tennenbaum. He approached her and shortly after took her on a trip to New York City to meet Wilhelmina Cooper, a former model who was running a modeling agency. Gia's success was immediate. Her exoticism represented a welcome and explosive break from the wholesome blondes who were in vogue at the time.

By the late 1970s and early 1980s, Gia's face and body were plastered across the pages of *Vogue* and *Cosmopolitan*. She was earning hundreds of thousands of dollars, and top photographers, such as Francesco Scavullo and Chris von Wangenheim, were clamoring to work with her. But as meteoric as her ascent had been, so too was her fall.

Drugs were prevalent in the fashion industry in which Gia worked and at the clubs she frequented. Although she used cocaine only recreationally at the start, she began turning to it more and more frequently. Constantly seeking the love and stability that had been denied her as a child, Gia used drugs to fill their absence. Wilhelmina Cooper, Gia's mentor, died in 1980 and Gia's relationship with makeup artist Sandy Linter did as well. Gia, devastated and anguished, turned to heroin to numb her pain. She was soon using up to four bags a day. She would walk out on shoots, arrive stoned or sometimes wouldn't arrive at all. Her moods swung wildly, and she often lashed out at those around her with violent tantrums, sometimes pulling out a switchblade when provoked.

Gia appeared in the November 1980 issue of *Vogue* with visible track marks on her arms. In 1982, Scavullo, the only photographer willing to work with her by that point, tucked her arms and hands behind her for a now-notorious cover photo. By 1986, Gia was nearly penniless, afflicted with AIDS and reduced to living in welfare hotels. She asked her mother to take her in but was refused. The two eventually reconciled, and Gia, lingering at Philadelphia's Hahnemann Hospital, finally had her mother's undivided attention. Gia Marie Carangi died on November 18, 1986. The fashion industry, which had adored and feted her just years before, wasn't even aware of her passing.

> Gia, devastated and anguished, turned to heroin to numb her pain. She was soon using up to four bags a day.

Making a film about Gia's life was a risky proposition,

Gia (1998)

full of the sort of edgy and gritty subject matter Middle America would prefer to ignore or to condemn. Jolie herself initially balked at taking the role (four times to be exact) because playing Gia would be daunting for her. Jolie told *Entertainment Weekly* that "Gia has enough similarities to me that I figured this would either be a purge of all my demons, or it was going to really mess with me." Ironically enough, Jolie thought little of the model. "I hated her," Jolie said, recalling the first time she saw Gia giving an interview on *20/20* in 1983, "she spoke with this affected accent and she was acting her butt off." (The interview was indeed notorious—though Gia claimed that she wasn't on drugs, the interview suggested the exact opposite.)

The similarities between the two women were obvious: both wrestled with self-esteem, both worked in professions that prize the aesthetic, and both came from broken and rootless childhoods. Playing Gia required Jolie to plumb the depths of her psyche, to explore her own demons and shadows and to tempt her heart of darkness. "I've definitely needed to learn the lessons Gia needed to learn," Jolie told *Entertainment Weekly*, "especially feeling that the physical is more important than anything else, or that you're only as smart and good as some-body thinks you are. It's been really important for me to look at myself in the mirror and realize that I can't let myself go down like she did."

Jolie lost herself in the role and found it particularly difficult to disengage. She entered a sort of exile in which she chose to "not do anything, not have friends, not visit, not hang out." The film-ing of *Gia* left her emotionally drained and Jolie wondered whether she had anything left of herself to give to her career. In an interview with *Rolling Stone*, she lamented, "I felt like I'd given everything I had and I couldn't imagine what else was in me." She swore off act-ing, a break catalyzed by the fact that she was still sporting

Jolie herself initially balked at taking the role (four times to be exact) because playing Gia would be daunting for her.

the shaved head required for Gia's final scenes. There were few roles, after all, for bald women.

Jolie then decided to enroll at New York University's film school and enjoyed, to a degree, the anonymity of the classroom. But still, the insecurities and terrors that had first plagued her as a teenager continued to stalk and haunt her. Like an anchor, they dragged her deep into depression, sapping the buoyancy of her spirit. She felt isolated, treading water in an ocean of unfamiliar and uncomprehending faces. The romanticism of the city had been dulled, seeming instead "cold, sad and strange." In her desperation, Jolie began feeling, once again, like "not wanting to be around anymore."

She seriously contemplated killing herself but again displayed an acute awareness of the guilt that suicide can foster in those closest to the victim. Therefore, to shield her family, Jolie decided to eschew the pills and knives and chose, instead, to hire a hit man to kill her. The killing would be staged as the final, desperate act in a robbery gone wrong. "I was very aware that so many people around me, like my mother, would feel as though they didn't give enough or do enough, if I'd taken my own life," she told *The Face* in 2003, "so my solution to it was if someone else had taken my life, then it would be murder and it wouldn't be that anyone would feel they'd let me down." But, in one of those epiphanous, truth-is-stranger-than-fiction moments, Jolie changed her mind.

She found a hit man (in New York you can find everything—he happened to be the friend of a friend) and decided that she would pay him in installments from her bank account so that she wouldn't draw unwanted attention. But the ironically optimistic hit man she contacted "spoke very sweetly to [her], and made [her] think about it for a month." After a month, events in Jolie's life led her to reexamine her life. "I figured I'd stick it out," Jolie said matter of factly to *The Face*. Not coincidentally, Jolie's about-face coincided with the raves she received for her turns in both *George Wallace* and *Gia*.

Having struggled for so long in projects that did not stimulate her, Jolie decided to turn her back on acting. Like everyone with a creative bent, Jolie sought to express and to communicate something through her work and to find validation for her efforts. Commercial and critical success certainly aren't the truest of barometers for creative success, but it certainly did not help that critics and others in the industry did not recognize the variety and scope of the roles she had chosen, nor the psychological underpinnings she had attempted to explore. As she told the *Chicago Tribune*, "If you have enough people sitting around telling you you're wonderful, then you start believing you're fabulous. Then someone tells you that you stink, and you believe that too." Reviews were monolithic in their assessment of her performances, and they often chose to focus more upon her aesthetic qualities.

However, *George Wallace* and *Gia* presented a complexity and depth to Jolie that few critics had noticed before and that few now could ignore. The overwhelming critical success of these two movies helped Jolie believe that perhaps she did have something to communicate, that there was something real and worthy in what she was doing. She also must have remembered the pact she had made with herself when she was 19 years old and ready to commit suicide in a New York hotel room—she decided to live every day as if it were her last. That

> **Having struggled for so long in projects that did not stimulate her, Jolie decided to turn her back on acting.**

creed goes a long way towards explaining both her seeming recklessness and impulsive instincts that have since fascinated the media.

But it isn't so much a recklessness that informs Angelina's life; rather, it is a fearless bent, a boldness and a thirst for experience that does so, and they are all, to a great degree, central to her popularity. How many among her fans and admirers would love, as she does, to cast off the shackles of everyday existence, seize every moment and every opportunity and live life as it was meant to be lived? Few can afford the liberation promised by such a philosophy, but through Jolie, they can sense it, smell it and taste it, however vicariously. For many it must be, and often is, enough.

chapter 6

A Dip in the Pool

George Wallace, airing over two August nights in 1997, premiered on the cable channel TNT and was an unqualified success. Critics lavished praise upon the miniseries that detailed the life of the controversial Alabama governor. With the largest popular vote in state history, Wallace ascended to the governorship in 1962, infamously proclaiming, "I draw the line in the dust and toss the gauntlet before the feet of tyranny, and I say, segregation now, segregation tomorrow, segregation forever."

On June 11, 1963, he appeared at the University of Alabama, determined to prevent the desegregation of that institution by blocking the entry of two black students, Vivian Malone and James Hood. Only when confronted by federal marshals did Wallace stand down.

For the next 15 years, Wallace played a prominent role in American politics as the face of the resistance to the civil rights movement, speaking against the advancement of black rights and of federal power. He ran for president four times, winning a surprising large number of votes in the 1964 Democratic primaries, and served as governor for four terms, in 1962, 1970, 1974 and 1982.

In 1972, Wallace was crippled for life when Arthur Bremer shot him during a campaign stop in Laurel, Maryland. Wallace was in and out of hospitals for the rest of his life and continued to experience agonizing pain from the bullet that had failed to kill him.

In the late 1970s, Wallace experienced something of a conversion. He became a born-again Christian and offered an apology for the segregationist views and racist policies he

> In 1972, Wallace was crippled for life when Arthur Bremer shot him during a campaign stop in Laurel, Maryland.

George Wallace (1997)

had supported throughout much of his career. In his final term as governor, the rehabilitated Wallace appointed a record number of blacks to government positions.

Directed by John Frankenheimer (*The Manchurian Candidate*), *George Wallace* rehabilitated a career rendered moribund by the simply bizarre and confusing *The Island of Dr. Moreau.* A deft blend of black-and-white and color, of archival footage and film, *George Wallace* won praise for its director and its cast. Gary Sinise, who came to the public's attention as the embittered Lieutenant Dan in *Forrest Gump* (1994) and as the stoic astronaut Ken Mattingly in *Apollo 13* (1995), crafted a complex, human and movingly sympathetic performance of Wallace as the film followed his rise to the governorship, his eventual rehabilitation and his three marriages.

Wallace's first wife was Lurleen Wallace, who was thrust onto the political stage when Wallace, seeking to circumvent Alabama's state constitution (which prevented him from running for a second term as governor), propped her up as a candidate. She won easily and was Alabama's first woman governor. Two years later, however, Lurleen Wallace died of cancer.

Three years after Lurleen's death, Wallace married Cornelia Snively, the niece of three-time Alabama governor "Big Jim" Folsom. Twenty years his junior and the divorced mother of two sons, Cornelia had known Wallace when she was seven years old, at which time he was serving as her uncle's aide. It was Cornelia who threw her body over Wallace's in the failed attempt on his life in 1972, and though she loved Wallace deeply, her filial obligations precipitated an acrimonious divorce in 1978 during which Wallace's lawyers painted her as a villain and left her nearly penniless.

> Jolie made her "out to be some silly, giddy Southern lady [who only] cared about shopping and buying clothes and making speeches for [Wallace]."

Jolie was cast as Cornelia, and she brought to the role a convincing southern accent and a fierce humanity with which Wallace was tempered. Cornelia presented a far richer and complex role than Jolie had previously undertaken; many in Alabama's political establishment viewed Cornelia with suspicion, questioning her motives.

Cornelia Wallace herself had little use for the film about her ex-husband. She said in an interview with *News Chief* that Jolie made her "out to be some silly, giddy Southern lady [who only] cared about shopping and buying clothes and making speeches for [Wallace]." The critics, however, were nearly unanimous in their praise of Jolie's performance and, in 1998, she was rewarded with a Golden Globe as Best Supporting Actress in a Series, Mini-Series or Motion Picture Made for Television. She also garnered an Emmy nod but ultimately lost to the equally spectacular Mare Winningham, who portrayed Wallace's long-suffering first wife, Lurleen. Gary Sinise was awarded an Emmy for his sterling efforts, and *George Wallace* went on to collect a Golden Globe as the Best Mini-Series or Motion Picture Made for Television.

The Golden Globes, awarded by the Hollywood Foreign Press Association (HFPA), had for years been maligned and dismissed as being meaningless. Its earliest critics pointed to the lax requirements for membership in the HFPA (many in the association worked in education, in real estate or in automobile sales) and accused the members of voting not for artistic merit but for the perks and attention they received from any given studio. Groucho Marx said of the association, "If they were willing to have me in it, I wouldn't want to join. I've always considered that joining [the HFPA] comes at a dreadful price—your credibility."

Some may have viewed Jolie's Golden Globe win as something less than a reflection of her acting ability but, beginning in the

1990s, the Golden Globes worked on rehabilitating its credibility by tightening membership requirements and restricting the gifts that studios could offer. In recent years, the awards have gained in prestige, acclaim and influence. By the late 1990s, they were already viewed as an often highly accurate barometer of the far more respected and coveted Academy Awards. The Golden Globe was then nothing less than the recognition of a fresh and fierce new talent.

Prior to the awards ceremony, which was held on January 18, 1998, at the Beverly Hilton Hotel, Jolie recalled being in a slight state of panic. She told Jay Leno in a 1998 interview that her shoes were too big, that her dress was see-through and that "it was just a big mess." The *Tonight Show* host, of course, voiced the opinion of most heterosexual men, and even women (such is the universal appeal of Jolie), when he asked why a see-through dress would be a problem. Jolie answered, as any daughter might, "My dad was there."

...when he asked why a see-through dress would be a problem. Jolie answered, as any daughter might, "My dad was there."

Accompanying Jolie at the awards were her brother, her mother and her father, who was nominated for his supporting role in *The Rainmaker* (he would lose to Burt Reynolds for his role as a pornography director in *Boogie Nights*). In her acceptance speech, a visibly elated and stunned Jolie thanked Gary

Screen Actors Guild Award (1999)

Sinise, praising him for being "brilliant, brave and amazing," John Frankenheimer and the Hollywood Foreign Press Association. She concluded, "And most of all my family. Mom stop crying, stop screaming. It's okay Jamie, my brother, my best friend I couldn't do anything without you. I love you so much. Dad, where are you? Hi. I love you. Thank you so much. Thank you."

Following the ceremony, Jolie celebrated her win by plunging into the Beverly Hilton Hotel pool and emerged, soaking, with her hand-beaded Randolph Duke gown clinging to her frame. So much for the bashful daughter who fretted that her dress might be too revealing. Photographers snapped away, but the moment had a deeper significance for the actress. As a child, she had done the same thing, only to be escorted off the hotel grounds. This time, there was no such ejection. She would not be denied the triumph of the moment.

She followed her dip in the pool by getting "really drunk," as she described to Conan O'Brien on *The Late Show*. Her father was with her, for at least a little while. "The first half of the night he was really proud of me," Jolie told O'Brien, "and then after I started downing tequila he

Following the ceremony, Jolie celebrated her win by plunging into the Beverly Hilton Hotel pool...

Golden Globe Award (1999)

was like, 'Oh, do you think that's a good idea?' and then he left. It was the last I saw of him."

On January 11, 1998, *Gia* premiered on HBO. Immediately, it was evident why Jolie felt as if she had given everything. She was fearless and bold, flawlessly embodying Gia's magnetism and ferocity. Critics were divided on the film itself—some found its portrayal of Gia's heroin addiction too didactic, while others found its pacing conventional and routine. Others praised the harrowing and grim film for its graphic and frank portrayal of Gia's self-destruction and failed relationship with her makeup artist.

> But whether or not they actually liked the film, critics were united in their praise for Jolie and the tragic power and raw emotion she brought to scenes depicting Gia's agonizing and brutal heroin withdrawal and her mugging and rape. Even those prurient reviewers who still found it necessary to point out Jolie's nude scenes found themselves mesmerized by her performance.

Jolie received a Screen Actors Guild Award for Outstanding Performance by a Female Actor in a Television Movie or Mini-Series for her work in *Gia*.

Immediately, it was evident why Jolie felt as if she had given everything. She was fearless and bold, flawlessly embodying Gia's magnetism and ferocity.

She also received an Emmy nomination for Outstanding Lead Actress. Also nominated that year in the same category were a host of acting giants: Judy Davis, Sigourney Weaver, Olympia Dukakis and Jamie Lee Curtis. But it was Ellen

Barkin who carried the day, winning for her role in *Before Women Had Wings*.

Jolie was also **rewarded** for her work in ***Gia*** with another **Golden Globe**, this time for **Best Actress**.

The triumphs of *George Wallace* and *Gia* pushed Jolie to the forefront of young actresses, but most importantly, these two movies helped to dispel the clouds of her depression. "I felt like someone who had crashed the party," Jolie said of her first Golden Globe win in an interview with *Rolling Stone* in 2001, "and suddenly it became easier for me to work. And then *Gia* came out, and people responded to it, and suddenly it seemed like people understood me. I thought my life was completely meaningless and that I would never be able to communicate anything and that there was nobody who understood…and then I realized I wasn't alone. Somehow life changed."

Acting and her life had meaning once again, and Jolie returned to acting and to film with renewed vigor. In just a few short years, she would find love again and garner that most coveted of acting acclaim, an Oscar.

hitting on
Hutton

Although Jolie found an audience eager and willing to embrace her on television, it was a different story on the big screen. In 1997, she co-starred in *Playing God*, a psychological thriller that blatantly and poorly aped the darkly funny and ironic overtones of Quentin Tarantino's brilliant and revolutionary *Pulp Fiction* (1994).

As acclaimed and groundbreaking as *Pulp Fiction* had been, it spawned a host of poor imitations that all failed to capture its wit, energy and brawny intelligence. Among these were 1997's *8 Heads in a Duffel Bag*, *Suicide Kings* (which never fully realized the potential of its promising storyline) and *Playing God*.

Playing God was directed by Andy Wilson, who had previously helmed episodes of the popular and gritty British series *Cracker*. It tells the story of disgraced surgeon Eugene Sands (David Duchovny, attempting to lay the groundwork for a career beyond Agent Fox Mulder in *The X-Files*), who was stripped of his license for operating on a patient while tripped out on amphetamines. The patient died, as did Eugene's career. Months later, Eugene spirals into drug addiction and spends his nights, and presumably his days, wandering the drug dens of Los Angeles looking to score synthetic heroin.

On one such evening, Eugene notices the stunning beauty, Jolie's Claire, but before the two can act upon their stolen glances, gunfire erupts. A man lies dying, and Eugene is the only man capable of saving his life. With a plastic bottle and some plastic tubing, Eugene improvises a breathing apparatus and saves the man's life. Watching it all with curiosity and awe is Claire, and so begins the tale of sacrifice and redemption.

Claire happens to be the girlfriend of counterfeiter and smuggler Raymond Blossom (Timothy Hutton, who first attracted critical notice in *Ordinary People* and *The Falcon and the Snowman* and then chose to eschew the Hollywood star-making machinery), and Raymond just happens to be looking for a surgeon of his own. Eugene is kidnapped and offered a deal with the devil. Raymond, fully aware of Eugene's own disreputable past, gives Eugene the chance to become a surgeon once again.

The work is less than savory, but Raymond wants to avoid the questions and paperwork that gunshot wounds in a hospital ER would solicit. With Eugene in his employ, Raymond can avoid all those tiny little hassles. Eugene grudgingly accepts Raymond's offer because it is his chance to be a doctor again, which is all he ever wanted, and he is quickly set up in a hotel room, complete with equipment and assistants. Indeed, in flashback, the audience learns that Eugene was only high during the 28-hour surgery that would prove to be his undoing simply because he needed to stay awake to finish his job. He wasn't looking for a fix; he was just dedicated to his work.

Matters of conscience aside, Eugene's situation is further complicated by his growing relationship with Claire and the arrival of an FBI agent who is keen to exploit the doctor and arrest Raymond once and for all. The premise is interesting enough, as are the inherent tensions of Eugene's position, and there is some black humor to be mined in Eugene's disgrace. Doctors, after all, are regularly expected to work for hours, perhaps days on end, and it's no surprise that Eugene resorted to such measures. But *Playing God,* for the most part, fell flat, becoming a kaleidoscopic mess of gore and ham-fisted dialogue.

Some critics did praise the film, notably Roger Ebert who found the film's plot grounded by its three leads. Ebert wrote that David Duchovny "has the psychic weight to be a leading man and an action hero" and compared him, perhaps a little overzealously, to Clint Eastwood and Robert Mitchum. As for Timothy Hutton, Ebert predicted a career resurrection that in the end failed to materialize (though Hutton did do a serviceable job in a small but pivotal role in 2004's *Kinsey*). And as Claire, Jolie had found "a certain warmth in a role that is usually hard and aggressive," stated Ebert. Other critics, however, were not so generous. One critic, rather harshly, deemed watching the film a "miserable experience…a time-waster…a piece of garbage," while another decried that there was nothing "ambitious or even entertaining about [the film]."

The film certainly wasn't the success its makers had envisioned, but it marked the last significant piece of work before Jolie's career broke through and the end, as well, of the relative anonymity she had enjoyed. True to her fashion, Jolie ended up dating one of her *Playing God* co-stars, Timothy Hutton.

Fifteen years older than Jolie, Hutton had first come to moviegoers' attention in Robert Redford's multi-Oscar-winning 1980 film, *Ordinary People*. For his sensitive, nuanced portrayal of Conrad Jarrett, the 20-year-old Hutton was rewarded with both a Golden Globe and an Oscar for Best Supporting Actor, and the film itself won Best Picture, Best Director and a Best Adapted Screenplay for Alvin Sargent (who would bring humanity and depth and win a whole new generation of fans to *Spider-Man 2*). Hutton's talent is

True to her fashion, Jolie ended up dating one of her *Playing God* co-stars, Timothy Hutton.

Playing God (1997)

best displayed in two films by Sydney Lumet: *Daniel* (1983) in which he played the son of Julius and Ethel Rosenberg, and in *Q & A* (1990).

Although some may consider Hutton's career to be unimpressive, given his substantial talents, he showed early in his career that he had an aversion to blatantly commercial projects. In fact, he was originally offered the lead role in **Risky Business** (1983), a part that went to the then relatively unknown Tom Cruise. **Risky Business** catapulted Tom Cruise into the stratospheres of stardom, and while agents and friends had pleaded with Hutton to accept the role, he staunchly refused and expressed no regrets in the aftermath of the film's success.

Some puzzled at the relationship between Jolie and Hutton because of their age difference. But looking at their histories, it's a little easier to understand why they found something attractive and familiar in the other. Like Jolie, Hutton was the child of an actor, the late Jim Hutton. Timothy had also acted, at the age of five, in a film with his father, and he had spent a childhood largely rootless. His parents divorced when he was three, and he spent the following years with his mother, shuffling between California, Massachusetts, and Connecticut. And, as with Jolie, Hutton knew the pain of love lost and the perils of negotiating a marriage under the pressures of the ever-watchful media

"I just haven't found that person to break through with...maybe some people don't find another person, you know?"

eye. His wife for four years had been actress Debra Winger. Hutton and Winger married in 1986 and divorced in 1990.

No one can say with any certainty what it was that drew Hutton and Jolie together, but they must have found an empathetic and comprehending soul within each other. The relationship may have provided some solace to Jolie while her marriage to Jonny Lee Miller limped along towards divorce. Ultimately, however, Jolie and Hutton stopped dating after a year. Two failed relationships following one another so closely might have led Jolie to swear off dating—as she had done so dramatically as a 16-year-old fresh from her first heartbreak—but she remained, instead, cautiously optimistic. "It should be a combination of thinking, 'I love you but I just want to rip that apart and eat you,'" she said. "I just haven't found that person to break through with…maybe some people don't find another person, you know?"

Reflecting upon her luck with love in 2000 with *Jane*, Jolie said, "I don't need to be with a person, but I do want to start a family. I mean, selfishly, it would make my life so much fuller, worth living. I'll have to have inspections [if I want to adopt]. People have said to me, 'You do the cover of *Rolling Stone* in a certain outfit and you talk about knives and being gay, the judge is going to see that. I'm the dark horse, so it's like suddenly…'" She didn't finished the thought. Jolie, who had for so long been candid with the press about her past, seemed to wonder whether she would have to compromise that liberation for the sake of filling the void in her life.

Indeed, in the coming years, her father, too, addressed the issue of whether Angelina would be a fit mother, resulting in the schism for which the father and daughter are noted today. But for the time being, Jolie was an ascending star. Following the success of her Golden Globe win for *Gia*, Jolie was being hailed by the press as the Next Big Thing, the It Girl (whatever It was and is, It must be huge), and she was watched closely as everyone wondered what her next project would be.

chapter 8

Scene-Stealer

Two films released in 1998, *Hell's Kitchen* and *Playing by Heart*, can't really be accurately called follow-ups to *Gia* because they had been filmed before the biopic's release and before Jolie's self-imposed exile from acting. But still, the two films do reflect her flourishing and growing talents.

In *Hell's Kitchen*, Jolie rises above a weak script and plodding story, while in *Playing by Heart*, she ably holds her own against the likes of Sean Connery and Gena Rowlands.

Hell's Kitchen deals with tough subject matter, exploring the blood-soaked and expletive-filled consequences of an old crime. Although the film premiered at the Toronto Film Festival in September 1998, it wasn't released in the United States until over a year later. The film was given a chilly reception in Hollywood North, and time did little to dispel the bad taste it left in audiences' mouths at its premiere.

In *Hell's Kitchen*, Johnny (Mekhi Phifer) is newly released from prison, having spent the past five years in jail for a failed robbery that led to the death of an accomplice, the brother of Johnny's girlfriend, Jolie's Gloria. Johnny, who is truly decent at heart, returns to the streets of New York and Hell's Kitchen, determined to become a professional boxer. Dreams, after all, are all he has left; his mother is dead and his younger brother has disappeared. He finds an eager mentor in Lou (William Forsythe), an ex-con and ex-champ trainer who, naturally, has a heart of gold.

Johnny's path to redemption, however, is littered with pitfalls.

In *Hell's Kitchen*, Jolie rises above a weak script and plodding story, while in *Playing by Heart*, she ably holds her own against the likes of Sean Connery and Gena Rowlands.

There is a crooked fight promoter, who happened to manage Lou many lifetimes ago, and a vengeful Gloria, who holds Johnny responsible for her brother's death and seeks to pay him out in kind. And there is also Patty (Johnny Whitworth), who, as an accomplice in the failed robbery, knows the truth of Johnny's innocence but whose lust for Gloria might just transform him into her messenger of death. Revenge, of course, is just another in the line of problems assailing Gloria. Her brother's death has left their mother (Rosanna Arquette) a strung-out, drug-addicted mess who falls clumsily into Patty's arms.

The film lurches from scene to scene, each staged with all the subtlety of a haymaker. The dialogue is heavy, hammering and relentless, and by the end, the viewer is left feeling pummeled and altogether weary. The only relief to be found is in the strong performances of both Mekhi Phifer and Jolie. Phifer had exploded on screen with his debut in Spike Lee's *Clockers* (1995) and found work equal to his talent as a modern-day Othello in *O* (2000) and as David "Future" Porter in *8 Mile* (2002). Jolie does what she can with the clichéd dialogue and overwrought plot that tries ever so gamely to attain operatic heights by slathering on the melodrama with a trowel. Thankfully, she was much better served in *Playing by Heart*.

Playing by Heart is an ensemble romantic dramedy, featuring a cast that included Sean Connery, Gena Rowlands, Ellen Burstyn, Madeline Stowe, Dennis Quaid, *The X-Files'* Gillian Anderson, Patricia Clarkson, Jay Mohr, Ryan Philippe (soon to be married

Playing by Heart (1998)

to another Next Big Thing, It Girl actress, Reese Witherspoon)
Anthony Edwards (then starring on NBC's popular *ER*) and Jon
Stewart. Multi-storied, with interlocking narratives that each
spin a different variation upon the movie's theme of love, *Playing by Heart* is the sort of film so unabashedly sappy and bright
in its exploration of love in all its permutations that you find
yourself smiling in spite of yourself.

Paul (Sean Connery) and Hannah (Gena Rowlands), married
for many years, avoid accepting the reality of Paul's inoperable
brain tumor by hiding in the discovery of a brief affair that
Paul had 25 years earlier. Meanwhile, Gracie (Madeline Stowe)
and Roger (Anthony Edwards) explore their own failed marriages through their shared infidelity and experience the ultimate emptiness of sex without love. Trent (Jon Stewart, in a
welcome departure from the smirks and preens of *The Daily
Show*) tries to woo Meredith (Gillian Anderson, worlds away
from somber Agent Scully), who'd rather not deal with a relationship, her own insecurities and the struggle to overcome the
limitations and impatience of love. Mildred (Ellen Burstyn)
attempts a bedside reconciliation with her estranged gay son
(Jay Mohr), who's dying of AIDS. Hugh (Dennis Quaid) is
unable to face who he really is and lures women to his bed with
fabricated tales of tragedy spun on barstools.

Jolie's extroverted, bold and open Joan tries to win over the
broody and private Keenan (Ryan Philippe). The stories all
eventually intersect as love and, for the most part, love triumphs. The film, of course, is far from realistic, but then again,
it's not trying to be, as noted when Joan says, "talking about
love is like dancing about architecture."

The studio's hopes for the film
couldn't have been very high
since *Playing by Heart* was
released in January, a typically
fallow period for films. Studios, fresh off the fall and
holiday releases of their
Oscar-baiting films, usually
offer smaller films as they wait
impatiently for the opening of

> Jolie's extroverted, bold
> and open Joan tries to
> win over the broody
> and private Keenan
> (Ryan Philippe).

the summer blockbuster season. Even though *Playing by Heart*'s audience was small, critics were kind to the film. Stephen Holden of *The New York Times* called it a "likably sappy romantic comedy," and James Berardinelli deemed it an "enjoyable diversion."

The movie did feature some admirable acting from fine actors, but it was Jolie who reaped much of the attention. Stephen Holden also noted that "for all its artificiality, [the film] has an earnest charm…much of that sweetness emanates from Ms. Jolie, who conveys the vulnerability beneath the hard-shell glamour of a restless leonine beauty prowling the L.A. singles scene." Charles Taylor of Salon.com called her performance "flabbergasting," and said that "Jolie appears to be unembarrassed by emotion…she leaps right into a part and somehow manages to filter out the calculation." He added, poetically, that "everything about her—eyes, cheeks, lips—seems full, ripe bursting with energy, and she talks with the speed of a buzz saw, but a buzz saw that purrs."

> Jolie explained that she accepted the role because Joan had a "very, very open kind of personality who just had no darkness, really, and was just very, very positive, and wanting love, and kind of kooky and fun and up all the time and colorful. For me, there is nothing in me that is normally like that or doesn't find that annoying."

Jolie eventually found a way to connect with the character through childhood remembrances of days when, as a four-year-old, she enjoyed just "making people laugh and wearing glitter underwear." It must have been a pleasure for Jolie to return to the carefree innocence of her earliest days and to escape, if for just a while. The obvious joy of portraying Joan's eternal optimism and blind faith in love reveals itself in Jolie's crackling energy and shimmering luminosity.

Acting rekindled the flame of Jolie's resolve and spirit, and these two films demonstrate how much acting needed her and how much she needed acting. In this art, Jolie discovered a reason to persevere. "I desperately need to communicate with people through films," she once said. "It's why I'm alive. Films are my therapy."

return
from Exile

The double successes of *George Wallace* and *Gia* pretty much guaranteed that Jolie would have a busy shooting schedule in 1998 in the sort of high-profile productions that had eluded her thus far. Her successes also intensified the glare of the media spotlight. In an *E!* interview, Jolie downplayed her own hype, saying, "I really don't take that stuff seriously." Presciently, she added, "I'm a really weird, goofy, odd little person, and people will discover that eventually. I'm a completely goofy person."

Of course, her definition of goofy appears not to be universal—her rising fame placed every aspect of her life under intense scrutiny, and her goofiness was construed as eccentric, weird and simply bizarre. It would all come to a head with her Academy Award win, her notorious acceptance speech and her infamous marriage to Billy Bob Thornton, an actor with quirks and peculiarities rivaling her own. For the moment, however, Jolie thrust herself into her work.

Major producers and directors now took notice of the actress and clamored to have her in their films. Martin Bregman, producer of *Scarface*, *Serpico* and *Carlito's Way*, had seen Jolie in both *George Wallace* and *Gia* and hailed her as being perhaps the "best actress to come down the pike in maybe the past 20 years."

Bregman subsequently cast her in *The Bone Collector* (1999), a suspense thriller in which two agents race to unravel the identity of a New York City serial killer. Jolie was also cast in two other very different productions: *Pushing Tin*, a dark comedy about the chaotic world of the air-traffic controller and *Girl, Interrupted*, an adaptation of Susanna Kaysen's memoir of her stint in a mental institution following an attempted suicide.

It was a busy year for Jolie, a year that gave her immense satisfaction, both personal and private. Through her work, Jolie rediscovered love in the similarly tattooed arms of Billy Bob Thornton on the set of *Pushing Tin*, and she received her first Oscar for her work in *Girl, Interrupted*. It has often been said that it is darkest before the dawn, and this was certainly true for Jolie. Disconsolate, suicidal and alone after the filming of *Gia*, Jolie now possessed everything that had seemed so eternally out of reach.

Pushing Tin marked Jolie's return to acting after her self-imposed retirement. Inspired by an article in *The New York Times* about air-traffic controllers working in the chaos of the New York Terminal Radar Approach Center, Art Linson (the producer of films such as Michael Mann's grossly underrated crime drama, *Heat*, and Cameron Crowe's sweet ode to *Singles*) optioned the rights to the story and turned to writers Glen and Les Charles to craft the script. The Charles brothers had scored great successes in television, creating the much-loved sitcom, *Cheers*, and their script caught the weary eye of director Mike Newell.

Newell, who had introduced American audiences to a bumbling and hopelessly charming Hugh Grant with *Four Weddings and a Funeral*, had just finished shooting the beautifully restrained mobster drama *Donnie Brasco*. Another shoot wasn't exactly what he had in mind, but the script and concept proved intriguing, and after rewrites that shifted the focus from the skies to the collisions between its characters, Newell agreed to take it on. To play the lead in the film, Newell wanted only one actor—John Cusack.

Cusack is one of those rare breeds of actor—a talented performer who shunned the spotlight and also managed to transition himself, with ease, from the youth-oriented roles with which he rose to prominence. His rise coincided with that of the well-known Brat

"I'm a really weird, goofy, odd little person, and people will discover that eventually. I'm a completely goofy person."

Pack. When he was 17 he had starred with Rob Lowe and Andrew McCarthy in *Class*, and with Brat Pack ingénue Molly Ringwald and go-to outsider Anthony Michael Hall in John Hughes' *Sixteen Candles*. Cusack quickly distanced himself from the Brat Pack, never enjoying the superstardom accorded to its members, but was also happily immune from their rapid descent into obscurity.

Instead, Cusack continued to take on the offbeat and underdog roles that suited him so well. He cemented a place in filmgoers' consciousness with his turn as the aspiring kick boxer and hopeless, boom-box-wielding romantic Lloyd Dobler in Cameron Crowe's sweet but never saccharine *Say Anything....* This was followed up by parts in John Sayles' *Eight Men Out* and Stephen Frears' *The Grifters*, after which he focused on productions for The New Criminals, a theater group he founded in 1988. He returned to the screen in 1997 with the well-received *Grosse Pointe Blank*, a film that he co-wrote and that was developed by his company, New Crime Productions. He then had roles in *Con Air* (a rare turn in a blatantly commercial blockbuster), *Midnight in the Garden of Good and Evil* and the marvelously twisting and mind-bending *Being John Malkovich*. His career was experiencing something of a resurgence, and it was at this time that he was asked to play Nick Falzone in *Pushing Tin*.

Rounding out the cast in *Pushing Tin* was Cate Blanchett, the Australian actress who had scorched screens with her Oscar-nominated performance as Queen Elizabeth I in Shekhar Kapur's period drama *Elizabeth*. Blanchett continued to stir the souls of audiences worldwide as Galadriel in Peter Jackson's staggering opus, *The Lord of the Rings*. Also in the cast, as everyone with a thirst for gossip knows, was Billy Bob Thornton, fresh off a second Academy Award acting nomination for his role as the harried brother in Sam Raimi's dark film *A Simple Plan*. And, in one of life's many ironies, Jolie was cast as Mary Bell, the wife of Thornton's antagonist, Russell Bell.

Pushing Tin opened on April 23, 1999, to mixed reviews, but whatever critics thought about the film's initially promising story, they quickly ran out of superlatives to shower upon its cast. The film is essentially a riff on the sort of one-upmanship alpha males live for. Nick Falzone (John Cusack), tightly wound and edgy, is the best air-traffic controller in New York's Terminal Radar Approach Control (TRACON) who only wishes he could direct his insecurities and paranoia as well as he directs the blips on his radar console. His lofty status is challenged when stone-cold maverick newcomer, Russell Bell (Thornton), arrives.

Preternaturally cool and composed, Russell is the sort of aggra-vating fella whose mastery and skill seem to come effortlessly. He maneuvers planes perilously close to one another, in what appears to be a preening display of machismo, but which is, upon closer inspection, actually a carefully devised system mar-rying speed and safety, the better to bring flights in on time. At a weekend barbecue outside of TRACON, Russell calmly eclipses Nick's record of shooting baskets. And just to complicate mat-ters further, Bell is accompanied by his young, curvaceous and hard-drinking wife, whose entrance causes the collective jaw-dropping of Bell's colleagues. In a moment of ironic resonance, one of the characters asks of Mary Bell, "What the hell is she doing with Russell?"

Nick is drawn to Mary Bell, not only because she represents escape from the middle-class suburban hell he shares with his wife, the stoic and underestimated Connie (Cate Blanchett), but also because she's married to Russell. Nick and Mary Bell fall into each other's arms just as Connie finds herself wondering what it is, exactly, that she finds so hopelessly intriguing about Russell. The promising setup, designed to ratchet up the ten-sions in an already tense TRACON, flails towards the end as potential disasters loom large and are averted. Ultimately, the film is compelling not for its novel story but for its four leads.

Although Washington has suffered from the criticism that he rarely strays from the stoic and quietly noble characters that have defined his career, this criticism is a thin and weak barb—one need only look to his glory-seeking and tortured Jake Shuttlesworth in Spike Lee's underrated *He Got Game* and his incendiary and scathing Oscar-winning performance as Alonzo Harris in Antoine Fuqua's otherwise drably conventional *Training Day*.

The Bone Collector presented a unique challenge for Washington, who met with dozens of spinal cord specialists and also with actor Christopher Reeve in order to better understand and portray a man paralyzed, from the neck down, save for one digit. Washington, propped up by pillows and bedridden for the shoot, forced Jolie to adapt. "It subdues your movement when you're with someone who can't move," she said of acting opposite Washington. "I naturally didn't touch his bed or move out of his eye line. You find yourself being stuck."

Released on November 5, 1999, *The Bone Collector*, which had been marketed as a suspense thriller along the lines of *The Silence of the Lambs*, didn't come close to matching that film's intelligence and depth. Philip Noyce, who had directed with cool efficiency the adaptations of Tom Clancy's *Patriot Games* and *Clear and Present Danger*, lingered on the mutilated bodies with their open wounds and rodent-denuded limbs, seemingly only to induce nausea in the viewer.

The plot revolves around the paralyzed Rhyme, a forensic specialist brought out of his own self-pitying somnambulism by what appears to be the work of a serial killer. The brutal crimes, in which victims are found trussed up and mutilated, have mystified officials and their only hope of catching the killer rests with Rhyme. The cat-and-mouse game becomes a race not just against time, but also

Angelina admitted to "throwing up," disgusted and horrified by "how one person could do such brutal things to another."

The Bone Collector (1999)

Rhyme's own failing body that is subject to violent seizures, any of which might prove fatal. Therefore, Rhyme enlists the help of policewoman Amelia Doughy. The film, though it contains moments of genuine terror and intelligence, collapses under the weight of its own absurd conclusions, and the gratuitous scenes designed to shock and to horrify only multiply the film's grim and humorless tone to a numbing degree.

If a reason is needed to view *The Bone Collector*, it would lie in its two leads: Denzel Washington and Angelina Jolie. Washington's talents are hardly challenged with the material, but his Rhyme is a constant pleasure to watch. Noyce compensates for the actor's immobility by focusing upon Washington's face, where his glints and gleams are more than sufficient to overcome his character's physical limitations.

Jolie, picking her way through the carnage of one crime scene after another, proves as illuminating as the ubiquitous flashlight with which her detective navigates the darkness. She is subtly restrained, bringing a grace and understatement to a film that needed far more of it. In her scenes with Washington, the two simmer with a mutual professional respect and a love that, obviously, can never be physically consummated. The chemistry between the two is palpable, far more alive and electric than anything else in the story.

Reviewers of the film could not dismiss the actors' shared charisma, and Jolie rightfully earned this comment from Salon.com reviewer Stephanie Zacharek: "Even as *The Bone Collector* plods on, fixating on each dingy or bloody detail, Jolie infuses the picture with a kind of grace. In the midst of all its ugliness, she alone shows any understanding of the rag and bone shop of the heart."

The strong, positively glowing reviews Jolie received for her work in *Pushing Tin* and *The Bone Collector* only confirmed her status as the Next Big Thing in Hollywood. *Girl, Interrupted* would cement it.

chapter 11

lisa on
her Mind

in 1967, 18-year-old Susanna Kaysen attempted suicide by ingesting 50 aspirin pills. The commitment wasn't total as she made a phone call beforehand that allowed her to get help in time for doctors to pump the pills from her stomach. She visited a psychiatrist a short time later who convinced her to admit herself to Boston's McLean Psychiatric Hospital, an institution famed for its treatment of so-called "graduates" Ray Charles and tortured poets Sylvia Plath and Robert Lowell. For the next two years—her stay funded with the money her parents had originally earmarked for college—Kaysen existed in a "parallel universe" of the insane.

She was diagnosed with borderline personality disorder, a condition marked by overwhelming doubts about an individual's self-image, which leaves the individual feeling empty and, often, suicidal. Relationships with others are usually fractious and tempestuous because individuals attach themselves quickly to friends but are disappointed when their great demands aren't met.

Given Kaysen's diagnosis (which seems to describe almost every young individual), it's not surprising that she found herself questioning the very efficacy of her treatment and that, 25 years later, she would explore and detail her two-year stint at McLean in her well-received and acclaimed memoir, *Girl, Interrupted*.

Intrigued by the very thin line that often separates madness from sanity, Kaysen wondered how her gender played a role in her diagnosis and institutionalization. And perhaps there was just the very real possibility that her sadness and confusion were far from the manifestations of some personality disorder but were, in fact, nothing more symptomatic of a teenager with a highly realized interior life. What is normalcy? What is deviancy? What is absurd and what is logical? These are the questions that inform Kaysen's darkly funny, scathingly insightful and humane memoir.

It is a recollection of her fellow patients (Daisy and her fixation on laxatives and chicken, and Susan with her penchant for wrapping everything she could lay her hands on in toilet paper), her doctors and the staff, her "keepers." The book was praised in the press, and when actress Winona Ryder read it, she began a four-year quest to bring the memoir to film.

Gamine actress Winona Ryder, like Jolie, had been one of Hollywood's up-and-comers and had easily met the expectations foisted upon her. The goddaughter of famed LSD advocate Timothy Leary, she grew up on a northern California commune, though her name betrays her Minnesota roots.

When she was 10, Ryder and her family moved to Petaluma, a community just outside San Francisco. Shortly after, she enrolled in acting classes at the American Conservatory Theater. In 1986, her failed audition tape for the film *Desert Bloom* caught the eye of director David Seltzer, and he subsequently cast her in the Corey Haim vehicle, *Lucas*.

Ryder then followed with a succession of the outsider and quirkily offbeat roles that have endeared her to a generation of fans: *Beetlejuice* and *Heathers*. In 1990 she teamed again with *Beetlejuice* director Tim Burton in his modern fable, *Edward Scissorhands*. The film propelled both Ryder and its lead, Johnny Depp, to stardom. The press, however, often ignored the actors' abilities and focused instead on the romance they kindled on

> The book was praised in the press, and when actress Winona Ryder read it, she began a four-year quest to bring the memoir to film.

set. The couple split and, in an oft-repeated tale, Depp altered a tattoo that once read "Winona Forever" to "Wino Forever."

Although Ryder could easily have become typecast, she demonstrated her range to great effect in Martin Scorsese's *The Age of Innocence* (for which she garnered her first of two Oscar nominations), became the Gen-X starlet of choice in *Reality Bites* and moved audiences to tears in *Little Women* (for which she earned a second acting nomination). Following the phenomenal success of *Girl, Interrupted*, which Ryder executive produced, her career entered a fallow period and it has yet to recover.

Her career had been marred both by blatantly commercial films (*Alien: Resurrection, Autumn in New York* and *Mr. Deeds*) and by the infamous shoplifting incident at Saks. The latter event induced the sort of gossip and rumor-mongering that plagued her following her retreat from *The Godfather III* (many whispered concerns that she had a drug problem) and the revelation that she was also carrying pharmaceuticals without a prescription only exacerbated the matter further.

> **Ryder revealed in the early 1990s that she had vacated her role in *The Godfather III* because once she had arrived on set in Rome, she found it impossible to get out of bed. Rumors to the contrary (Was it drugs? Was it Johnny Depp?), Ryder had voluntarily checked herself into a mental hospital, unable to cope with a succession of overwhelming anxiety attacks.**

When she read *Girl, Interrupted*, as a 21-year-old in 1993, the actress found within it a resonance and honesty that mirrored her own anxieties, concerns that she had been unable to voice to anyone—not to her family, not to her therapist. She was determined to bring the book to screen in the hopes that it would help others to know that they weren't alone with their insecurities. "Since I've talked about my anxiety," she said in an interview with *Entertainment Weekly*, "I've gotten a really good response. Young women were grateful to learn that it happens to everybody, even to people they consider perfect people with perfect lives." It was a tortured path.

When Ryder attempted to option Kaysen's book, she discovered that producer Doug Wick had already done so, to the great discontent of studio Columbia Pictures. It wanted to shy away from the project, seeing little marketable in the material's dark humor, complicated female characters and lack of a plot. But Wick persevered, and when Ryder contacted him, expressing her interest in the project and her desire to play Susanna Kaysen, he suddenly had a star who stirred the interest of Columbia.

Ryder called director James Mangold, who had handled matters of insecurity before. In his debut film, *Heavy*, he had chronicled the loneliness and weariness of an obese pizza maker, henpecked by those around him into a numbing and depressing silence. "Big as an ox, but nobody sees you," a customer remarks to the pizza chef as he shuffles quietly around the kitchen. *Heavy* was a critical favorite and won the grand jury prize for best direction at the Sundance Film Festival. As a writer and director, Mangold plumbed with eloquence the depths of isolation and loneliness. Ryder had seen the film and felt Mangold possessed the sort of touch that made him the ideal candidate to helm her project.

Mangold, just wrapping up work on *Cop Land* (another Sylvester Stallone stab for the credibility he had long ago squandered after his undeniably powerful work in *Rocky* and *First Blood*), agreed to direct, but he wanted permission to rewrite the script. The screenplay had already passed through the hands of three different screenwriters, which is never a good sign. Mangold, for his part, related to *Entertainment Weekly* his fear "that the project was headed to a touchy-feely Lifetime movie. I wanted to make a woman's picture with balls." To do so, he reorganized many of the

When she read *Girl, Interrupted*, as a 21-year-old in 1993, [Ryder] found within it a resonance and honesty that mirrored her own anxieties...

book's events in an attempt to vest it with a more linear and coherent narrative, and he also invented characters and situations not present in the memoir.

> He worked on the screenplay for a year, arriving at an epiphany when he read Salman Rushdie's essay on **The Wizard of Oz**. He knew then that he would structure **Girl, Interrupted** like Dorothy's journey into Oz, an escape into a universe where no one is whole. Ryder loved Mangold's work, claiming that unlike other directors approached for the project, he just "got it."

When Jolie heard about the project, she knew immediately that she had to be in the film. She even had her role picked out: Kaysen's volatile ward mate, Lisa Rowe. Jolie, like Ryder, was already a huge fan of the book, but given the book's subject matter, her reaction is not a surprise. She understood all too well the fragility of self-esteem and the desire to escape and to end it all. "I'd read the book years before and had underlined most of my character," she said in an interview with *Entertainment Weekly*. "I loved her and identified with her."

For an actress who viewed her roles as her own private form of therapy, here then was the filmic equivalent of Prozac. Lisa, according to an interview Jolie had with *E!*, "was all about instinct, a complete sociopath with no emotion and no sensitivity. And so, it was a way of tapping my insides." She begged for the role and, given her recent successes, it came as no shock that she was cast as the volatile and charismatic Lisa Rowe.

In fact, Ryder had recommended Jolie to Mangold after watching *Gia*. When Mangold met with Jolie, he had already auditioned several actresses but none seemed capable of playing the "Jack Nicholson in drag" he'd envisioned when penning the script. Then in walked Jolie. "She sat down," said Mangold, "and was

Lisa. I felt like the luckiest boy on earth." Originally asked to read just two scenes, Jolie proceeded to read every scene that contained Lisa. Mangold was fascinated. "I was exhausted afterwards," he said, "but I also knew she was going to be Lisa. It was the first moment where I felt like I actually had a movie."

The film was shot in early 1999 in Harrisburg, Pennsylvania, as the actors and crew decamped to film in an actual mental institution. The shoot proved taxing for all but especially for the actors. Ryder described how she was often unable to rein in her emotions after Mangold had yelled cut, saying that "to play an anxiety attack, you have to get an anxiety attack. And I didn't know how to put a lid on that. My heart would still be going a million miles an hour, and I would be sweating, and I would feel like I felt when I was 19 and felt totally alone and couldn't describe to anyone in the world how I was feeling." It was an experience not unlike that of Jolie's.

To more accurately portray the unsympathetic and cold Lisa Rowe, Jolie recalled how when Ryder told her about her tough day or how she wasn't feeling well because of a headache, Jolie told her co-star that she didn't and couldn't know that. "As Lisa, I can't know that," she explained. "I needed to not feel things. I need to not feel as if were all together. I needed to feel nothing." The two never really got acquainted; it was only on the rare occasion that the actresses shed the skin of their roles.

So firmly entrenched was Jolie in her character that she made few friends with the cast of young actresses. Brittany Murphy, of *8 Mile* and *Clueless*, was cast as Daisy, a socialite who exists strictly on a diet of chicken and laxatives. In the script, Daisy is

Girl, Interrupted (1999)

often maligned at the hands of a disapproving Lisa. "There was one night," Murphy said, "when I saw [Angelina off-set]. We were actually talking for a while. And then she said, 'Wait a minute—what am I talking to you for?' I said, 'Can't we take a break for a while?'" Murphy recalled that Jolie simply laughed and that was when Murphy knew that the conversation was over.

> Jolie feared that filming **Girl, Interrupted** would be a very dark time and admitted that "in some ways it was." But, at the same time, there was a sense of liberation about it all. "I lived completely on impulse," she said. "If I wanted to kiss someone, I did, and if I wanted to throw something, I could."

The final cut of the film, however, puzzled Jolie. While watching it, she worried that her character had been vilified and rendered wholly unsympathetic. In *Entertainment Weekly*, Jolie spoke of how throughout the shoot, she had seen her character as "a really positive force…as someone very much deserving of compassion." Mangold's edits, in Jolie's eyes, robbed Lisa of her dignity and oversimplified her institutionalization. "I saw her for who she was," Jolie said. "So that's why I hate to think that it's seen as [right] for people like her to be locked up."

Mangold stood firmly behind his cuts, stating simply, "Nothing would have changed the way you perceive the movie. I wrote the scene, I shot it, but when I included it the energy of the film dies, so it was cut. It's just part of the process of making a movie."

Given its cast (Oscar-nominated Ryder and Golden Globe winner Jolie), rising director (Mangold) and critically acclaimed source material, it's little wonder that Columbia Pictures had high hopes for *Girl, Interrupted*. The film was released on December 21, 1999, a slot reserved for movie studios' Oscar-baiting releases. Expectations were, understandably, lofty.

Girl, Interrupted (1999)

The film received decidedly mixed reviews, with the strongest among them proclaiming it "shrewd, tough, and lively—a junior-league *One Flew Over the Cuckoo's Nest*," while the most scathing reviews accused the film of "tired conventions, hoary themes and obvious conclusions."

Infamously of all, Susanna Kaysen herself felt that the movie as a whole, in spite of Ryder's performance, had faltered and swore off films for a year (she had visited Harrisburg during filming and said that Ryder "had claimed [the role]" and was duly impressed with her fanatical dedication).

In the film, when Kaysen (Winona Ryder) is admitted to Claymoore after her aborted suicide attempt and diagnosed with borderline personality disorder, it is the supervising nurse (Whoopi Goldberg) who accurately susses out exactly what's bothering Kaysen: "You are a lazy, self-indulgent little girl who is driving yourself crazy." Unwilling or unable yet to leave her own girlhood behind, Kaysen quickly and easily finds herself a place within Claymoore's collection of mentally disturbed patients, discovering within their fractured souls a measure of comfort and escape.

The patients included self-mutilating burn victim Polly (Elisabeth Moss); laxative and rotisserie-chicken-loving, rich girl Daisy (the always delightfully unhinged Brittany Murphy who will, to her discredit, always be remembered as the girl Ashton Kutcher left for

Jolie takes what could have easily been a one-note and archetypal role and embraces the character so fully and blithely that her Lisa becomes the elemental soul of *Girl, Interrupted*...

Demi Moore); and *The Wizard of Oz* fanatic Georgina (an open and wonderful Clea Duvall, much better served here than in *She's All That* and *The Faculty*).

Most intriguing of all is Jolie's sociopathic so-crazy-she-might-be-sane Lisa, whose naked aggression and blunt honesty initially feel like liberation to Susanna from the values and hypocrisies of her well-to-do family. In time, the two become enemies; Susanna arrives at the inevitable conclusion that Lisa just might not be the best role model to emulate after all.

Girl, Interrupted was ostensibly a vehicle for Ryder, but her grace, coolness and wide-eyed curiosity were trumped by Jolie's frenzied charisma, confidence and combustible energy. Jolie takes what could have easily been a one-note and archetypal role and embraces the character so fully and blithely that her Lisa becomes the elemental soul of *Girl, Interrupted*—its raging id. Jolie's work immediately had Hollywood tongues uttering Oscar. Her third Golden Globe nomination and subsequent triumph over Catherine Keener, Samantha Morton, Chloë Sevigny and Natalie Portman all but assured Jolie of an Oscar nomination.

chapter 12

A Date with Oscar

On January 23, 2000, the 57th Golden Globe Awards were presented. The first award to be handed out that evening was to the winner in the excessively wordy category of Best Performance by an Actress in a Supporting Role in a Motion Picture: Angelina Jolie. For the third year in a row, Jolie had captured a Golden Globe. Her hair an odd shade of gray, Jolie accepted the award, clutching the arm of her brother, a portent of things to come.

"I had to bring my brother up here," she said in her acceptance speech. "He just had to see the view from up here. This means so much to me because this film means so much to me. The experience of it…exposing ourselves to each other and taking care of each other, that's really what we should be doing every day. Thank you so much for letting me be free and telling me it's okay. Winona [Ryder], thank you so much for all your hard work…you should be up here with me. The Foreign Press—thank you. You guys are so kind to me. I must be paying you or something."

The Golden Globe win, often a foreshadow of the Oscar nominations, virtually guaranteed that Jolie would be attending the 2000 Academy Awards ceremony. As rewarding as the Golden Globe had been for Jolie, the dearth of other nominations for *Girl, Interrupted* were ominous signs indeed.

When the Academy Award nominations were announced a month later, *Girl, Interrupted* had been shut out of nominations in all the major categories. It proved poor competition in the face of Sam Mendes' dystopic *American Beauty*,

In just three years, she had collected three Golden Globes and an Oscar; some actors take years to accumulate that sort of hardware.

Michael Mann's tense drama *The Insider*, M. Night Shyamalan's twisty audience-pleaser *The Sixth Sense*, and Spike Jonze's eccentric and brain-bending *Being John Malkovich*. *Girl, Interrupted* scored a single nod, and it amazed no one to hear that Jolie had been nominated for Best Supporting Actress. She was in good company.

Also nominated that year were Toni Collette for **The Sixth Sense**, Catherine Keener for **Being John Malkovich**, Chloë Sevigny for **Boys Don't Cry** and Samantha Morton for **Sweet and Lowdown**. It was a distinguished list to be sure, but many observers felt that it would be an upset if anyone other than Jolie walked away with the trophy.

The 72nd Academy Awards were presented on March 26, 2000. James Coburn, who had won for Best Supporting Actor the year before for his turn in *Affliction*, announced Angelina Jolie as the winner of the Oscar for Best Supporting Actress. Accompanied by her brother, Jolie took a moment to compose herself before walking on stage to accept the award. She cut quite a fearsome figure: she was clad in black, her eyes were rimmed with thick, black eyeliner and her blacker than black hair framed her face like a mane. She was visibly excited and awed as she graciously began her acceptance speech. "God, I'm so surprised no one's ever fainted up here," she said. "I'm in shock. And I'm so in love with my brother right now. He just held me and said he loved me. And I know he's so happy for me…Winona, you're amazing. And Whoopi, everybody. My family for loving me. Geyer Kosinski [her manager], my mom who's the most brave, beautiful woman I've ever known. And my dad, you're a great actor, but you're a better father. And Jamie. I have nothing without you. You're the most amazing man I've ever known, and I love you." She broke down in tears before leaving the stage.

The moment was undeniably a watershed moment in the actress' young career and a measure of how far she had come. In just three years, she had collected three Golden Globes and an Oscar;

some actors take years to accumulate that sort of hardware. But in what should have been a moment of celebration, the culmination of a childhood dream, her victory quickly turned sour.

When she accepted her Oscar, Jolie kissed her brother on his mouth. The buss, coupled with the praise she had showered upon him in her speech, took center stage and was dissected and debated endlessly in the media. Rumor-mongers whispered that perhaps Jolie was involved in an incestuous relationship with her older brother, and the accusations proved hurtful and unfounded.

"It hurts when people just make light of things that are important to you," she lamented once. "Like taking your relationship with your brother, which is a very beautiful thing, and twisting it so your parents are watching the television, it's a moment they'll

remember forever and now rather than seeing a beautiful moment for their children, they're thinking, 'Oh, my God, the whole world is calling our children perverted publicly.'" The two siblings had always been close, not surprisingly, given their parents' divorce and a childhood spent constantly on the move in which the only certainties were their own company and familial love. Indeed, when Jolie had cut her hand on the set of *Pushing Tin*, it had been Haven who had escorted her to the hospital.

Jolie was called upon to defend her behavior. "I didn't snog my brother," she said emphatically. "I wanted an Oscar my whole life—my father had had one. Me and my brother had a very difficult upbringing. We both survived a lot together and it meant a lot that he supported me my whole life. And in that moment, you reach to kiss somebody, and you end up kissing their mouth. Who cares? It wasn't like we had our mouths open, it wasn't some romantic kiss."

In fact, the ignorant press wasn't aware yet that Jolie was madly in love with actor Billy Bob Thornton, a circumstance that allowed Haven to dismiss the rumors with a wave of his hand. In the end, however, Haven and Jolie did begin limiting their contact, neither wishing to feed the gossip mill and have their mutual love and respect distorted and misrepresented, tragic to be sure.

> **"They were always together, Jamie and Angie," said Voight. "They hung out together as a team. Angie cared so much for Jamie, and Jamie was always taking care of her. Jamie is the big brother...he's the superhero."**

The Oscar and the resulting publicity and fame marked a change in the media's treatment of Jolie. Whereas she had once been portrayed as a wild child, the notoriety of her acceptance speech and eventual marriage to Billy Bob Thornton led to her being cast in the media as weird, dark and eccentric.

all things

Billy

When Jolie appeared on *The Tonight Show* in early 1999, it was to promote her film, *Pushing Tin*. At one point, host Jay Leno asked her about working with her co-star, Billy Bob Thornton. Jolie then admitted to Leno that she enjoyed her kissing scenes with Billy Bob and that she found him both romantic and sexy.

The origins of Jolie's and Thornton's courtship and subsequent marriage read as if culled from a Nora Ephron script, replete with near-misses, murmurs of will they or won't they and moments of inspired serendipity. For years, Jolie and Thornton had shared the same manager, Geyer Kosinski. Naturally, they had heard about each other, and had even sat in the same room with one another but had never actually met. Kosinski had hinted at the prospect of setting the two

actors up, once mentioning off-hand and quite prophetically to Thornton, "There's this girl, and she's kind of like you as an actor. She's the female you. I'm afraid to introduce you because I'm afraid you'll get married." Jolie recalled, in a 2002 interview with *Vogue*, that their mutual manager had said, "Billy Bob's doing this and that, and you two are driving me crazy."

Jolie and Thornton finally met on the set of *Pushing Tin* in Toronto while riding the same elevator. They shook hands, exchanged greetings and immediately there were sparks. "I remember wishing the elevator had gone to China," Thornton told *Rolling Stone*. "It's like a bolt of lightning. Something different happened that never happened before." Jolie, similarly struck by a thunderbolt, felt disoriented and ended up walking into a wall. When Thornton asked if she wanted to accompany him as he tried on some pants, Jolie "nearly passed out. All I heard was him and taking off his pants."

Ironically, Jolie had been cast as Mary Bell, wife to Thornton's antagonizing and maverick air-traffic controller, Russell Bell and, just to further the "hmm" quotient, *Pushing Tin* was the first project Jolie accepted after her return to acting. The two had dinners together (though they were usually accompanied) and spoke often. After filming wrapped, the two didn't speak to each other for a while and when they did, it was only by phone. But something was there. Jolie said, "I knew that somebody exists that represents all things that I stand for and believe in." To commemorate their meeting, Jolie had Thornton's name tattooed on her groin.

Billy Bob Thornton, born in Hot Springs, Arkansas, on August 4, 1955, came from a world quite removed from that of Jolie's.

Growing up in the economically depressed and still segregated rural south, Billy Bob (named after his father and his maternal great-grandfather) grew up in abject poverty, living in a cabin with no amenities and subsisting on the game his family could catch in the wilderness. He read often, developing a fondness for the works of southern writers Flannery O'Connor and William Faulkner, and he began writing short stories of his own. As a teenager, Thornton played baseball, becoming a local star of sorts for his pitching. And with the sounds of his parents' Elvis Presley, Jim Reeves and Beatles albums ringing in his head, he also formed rock bands, all the while directing and acting in school plays and productions.

Thornton's early life was marred by tragedy. When he was 18, freshly graduated from high school, his father died at age 44

The Golden Globe Awards

after a lengthy battle with lung cancer (most likely caused by the years spent inhaling the toxic fumes at his factory job). During the last months of his father's life, Billy Bob was constantly at his side and often carried him to bed.

Thornton left Arkansas shortly thereafter and drifted through a number of jobs, performing with his band whenever he could and working as a roadie, a grocery store clerk, a painter and a drill press operator. His promising baseball career ended before it could even begin when an errant pitch broke his collarbone, scuttling hopes of playing for the Kansas City Royals.

In 1977, with his aspiring novelist friend Tom Epperson in tow, Thornton headed for New York City, determined to find a career as an actor. Their stay was short-lived, and the next year, Thornton and Epperson headed to Los Angeles, where Thornton bided time as he tried to decide between music and acting. The matter didn't really get settled, and he returned shortly after to Arkansas, where he married his first of four wives.

He studied psychology briefly at Henderson State University but in 1984 decided to make another go of it in California. It was a difficult time; Thornton's accent and name, so distinctly tied to his boyhood south, brought him few notices or roles. To support himself, he sold pens and worked for an answering service. He could afford to eat only potatoes, a diet that eventually landed him in hospital with myocarditis, an inflammation of the heart brought on by malnutrition.

However, a few months later, Thornton fully recovered and continued to audition. He gradually earned small television roles on series such as *Matlock* and *Knots Landing*. Frustrated with the lack of roles that appealed to him, Thornton created a one-man stage show that he called *Swine Before Pearls*, in which he developed and originated the character of Karl Childers, the role that would prove to be his breakthrough.

Writing appealed to Thornton, and one evening, while working as a waiter at an industry Christmas party, he started a conversation with an older gentleman who offered him some sound advice: focus on the writing, it'll help you find a niche. It was only moments later, in the kitchen, that Thornton learned that the old man who he had just spoken to was none other than

Billy Wilder, the revered writer and director of such classics as *The Apartment* and *Sunset Boulevard*. Thornton clung to Wilder's advice, and with his childhood friend, Tom Epperson, Thornton began writing scripts.

Their first script, *One False Move*, starring Bill Paxton (with whom Thornton would work again on Sam Raimi's dark and tragic *A Simple Plan*), was well received, and just as his writing career began to take flight, so too did his acting career. He guest-starred on a few episodes of the Burt Reynolds' sitcom, *Evening Shade*, and translated those guest spots into a supporting role in *Hearts Afire*, a sitcom that ran for three years. *Hearts Afire* starred the *Night Court* actress Markie Post and John Ritter, who would shed his comedic harried Everyman image to great effect in Thornton's *Sling Blade*.

In 1993, Thornton directed a short feature, *Some Folks Call It a Sling Blade*, which introduced cinema to Karl Childers. It was a success, and Thornton, seeking to develop and to explore the character further, returned to Arkansas in 1996 to direct his first feature-length film, *Sling Blade*. Despite his small budget, the film featured a talented cast of veterans, including mentor Robert Duvall (who had starred in Thornton's and Epperson's *A Family Thing*), J. T. Walsh and John Ritter and newcomers Lucas Black (who had first awed audiences in the under-appreciated television series, *American Gothic*) and country music star Dwight Yoakam, who astonished many with his searing turn as an abusive stepfather.

Speaking in just a rasp, his head clean-shaven, his lower jaw protruding like an extra appendage, Thornton disappeared wholly into Karl Childers. *Sling Blade* heralded the arrival of a significant acting, writing and directing talent. The film received multiple Academy Award nominations, including a nod for Best Actor, and won for Best Adapted Screenplay.

> Thornton, the actor who for years couldn't get cast because of his accent and name, was suddenly very much in demand...

Thornton, the actor who for years couldn't get cast because of his accent and name, was suddenly very much in demand, and over the course of the following years, would prove that *Sling Blade* had been no fluke. His talents are exceptional; he is the very definition of a chameleon, capable of playing both noble and stoic in the 1998 blockbuster *Armageddon*, disturbing and frightening in Oliver Stone's *U-Turn* (1998), and comedic and witty in *Primary Colors* (1998).

That Thornton is able to move seamlessly among roles with such apparent and relaxed ease is testament to his abilities, and the actor received another acting nomination from the Academy for his work as the harried brother of Bill Paxton in *A Simple Plan*. And then along came *Pushing Tin* and Jolie.

For Jolie, the reasons for the connection between her and Thornton were obvious. When she met Thornton on the set of *Pushing Tin*, she had stripped herself of all her facades. She was, as she puts it, "clearly just myself. Billy and I don't wear masks, so the two of us saw each other as who we were." It's Thornton, too, whom Jolie credited for helping her erase the remaining shreds of the depression and hopelessness that had haunted her since she finished work on *Gia*.

"I was one of those people who felt like I didn't really live in this world," she said in *Premiere*. "I was very dark, and just didn't have very much hope, didn't really settle, didn't think I'd ever feel grounded or centered or warm and safe. I thought I'd burn until I went out. And then I met Billy and it all changed. We have the same things that haunt us, maybe, in many ways. And I think we understand each other, and also we accept each other completely as we are. So nothing feels bad. It's like being with somebody who really wants me to be who I am and who lets me see who he is. And that just makes everything in life very real."

Reality gave Jolie strength, and the difference was especially visible to those who had seen the actress fall slowly to pieces while filming *Gia*. Following her Oscar win for *Girl, Interrupted*, Jolie flew to Mexico early the next morning, where she was filming *Original Sin* with actor Antonio Banderas and where she was also reunited with her *Gia* director, Michael Cristofer and most of the biopic's crew. Asleep in her trailer, she was roused from slumber by the sounds of a mariachi band that Cristofer and Banderas had hired to celebrate her victory. When she blearily stumbled from her trailer, Jolie found the cast and crew waiting for her, each of whom bore a single rose, which they then handed to her. When all was said and done, Jolie stood there with 200 roses in her arms. It was a poignant moment for her.

In a *Premiere* interview, Jolie spoke of how "everybody was emotional. It was kind of like I was their little girl. And I felt like the little girl was going to survive, maybe, this business. I'd been very fragile with all of them, and then [while shooting *Original Sin*] they saw me fall in love, and they saw me find a home. But they also knew me when I was really, really worried that I would just die young and have very little life. So it was amazing."

It was clear to all that Thornton had no small hand in the Jolie's transformation. Banderas saw that "it was very obvious that this girl was in love. When somebody's in love, you don't hide it. I was very happy for her because actually I like Billy. In the case of Angelina, at least for me, there is nothing to criticize. I feel the opposite: I congratulate them."

Jolie and Thornton were wed at the Little Church of the West and wore jeans in a ceremony that lasted just 20 minutes.

Indeed, many clucked their tongues at the prospect of a relationship between the 24-year-old Jolie and the 44-year-old Thornton. And though their connection was immediate, there was a slight catch. Thornton, at that time, was involved in a relationship with actress Laura Dern, while Jolie was still nursing her recent divorce from Jonny Lee Miller. Banderas knew all too well the perils of courting someone involved in a long-term relationship. After all, his relationship with Melanie Griffith had begun when the helium-voiced actress was married to 1980s pinup and *Miami Vice* star Don Johnson. Banderas' congratulations, then, came from a position of weariness, experience and a knowledge of how love is an unpredictable and gossamer-like thing, a gift not to be dismissed lightly and one that should be tasted to its fullest.

During the filming of *Original Sin*, Jolie would often fly to Los Angeles from Mexico to be with Thornton; though for the longest time, their relationship was strictly spiritual. They spent their stolen moments together just talking and exploring the topography of their shared emotional terrain. It was only mere weeks before their May 5, 2000 wedding in Las Vegas, Nevada, that the two became physically intimate.

Jolie and Thornton were wed at the Little Church of the West and wore jeans in a ceremony that lasted just 20 minutes. Although the news shocked many outsiders, as did the candidness with which both spoke of their union and sex life, it was undeniably clear that the two were truly, madly and deeply in love. But life lived under intense media scrutiny is never easy, and the press, to the couple's complete bewilderment, would savage the union.

In December 2000, just months after their marriage, *Movieline* named Billy Bob Thornton "Most Permanently in a Midlife Crisis" (a sobriquet no doubt given in light of Thornton's multiple marriages), and Jolie "Most Likely to Scare a Psychiatrist." In *New York* magazine, four gossip columnists spoke over dinner and when asked which celebrity they loved to gossip about, three out of four said Jolie. One said, "I'm always waiting to see what crazy, weirdo thing she does next," and then predicted that Jolie and Thornton's relationship would end and end soon. The columnists then discussed how long they thought the union would last, and the estimates were no longer than six months, with the shortest being four. It was all impossibly cruel, callous and catty.

It didn't help that the couple were brazen in discussing their love. Thornton once said, "I was looking at her sleep and I had to restrain myself from literally squeezing her to death. Sex for us is almost too much," to which Jolie responded, "You know how you love someone so much you can almost kill them?"

The couple was also prone to engaging in long kisses on the red carpet with their complementary tattoos on display and to wearing those notorious vials of their blood around their necks. For an anniversary, Thornton, to the great fascination of the press and public, had his own blood drawn and then used it to paint pictures for his wife; Jolie, for her gift, had bought Thornton a grave plot.

Thornton was portrayed as a kook; his fear of flying and of antiques were played up to dizzying degrees. So, too, was the fact that he signed a document in his own blood pledging never to leave Jolie, and then, of course, there was the message, "To the End of Time," written in Jolie's blood above their bed. Most infamously of all, Thornton admitted to wearing Jolie's underwear when she was away, and at the MTV Movie Awards in 2000, he told reporters that he and Jolie had "just f***ed" in their limo. There were even rumors that Thornton wouldn't eat anything that wasn't orange.

What is clear in all this is that any life lived under the microscope is bound to look odd and strange. As individuals, everyone has their own particular quirks and fancies, but they're rarely examined and magnified to the point that they become caricature. Thornton and Jolie, as celebrities, were denied that privacy. Instead, they were viewed with a mixture of suspicion and derision for actions that surely held greater personal significance, meaning and symbolism that only the two of them could ever fully understand.

"There are people who don't want us to be happy," Thornton told *Vogue*. "And I've never understood why somebody wouldn't want someone else to be happy. The thing is, we're not out to hurt anybody. I mean,

JOLIE FAN FACT

Billy Bob Thornton once presented Angelina with poodles as a gift; following their divorce, Angelina wanted nothing to do with them, calling them "a mistake."

honestly, we're soul mates. I don't know what else to call it. It sounds corny, but I don't know what else to say. I don't know why people wouldn't just say, 'Oh, great, that's fantastic,' even if they think we're freaks." Although many viewed the two as being diametrically opposed, Thornton claimed that it was the exact opposite.

In the *Toronto Sun*, he said, "According to most people, we are the least likely two people to make it, given our history of things like that. In fact, it's exactly the opposite. I was unfocused my entire life, and so was she. Now we're both very clear and very focused. It's like it takes one to know one. We saw each other and it was like, 'OK, finally everything makes sense.' For the first time in my life in a relationship, I'm not nervous." The two had found within each other an empathy and comprehension, and for the first time in a long while, Jolie had found a home for her heart.

"I'm calm with Thornton," Jolie told *Premiere*, "I've found that I can be really soft. And I never was before. When I go home, I can really breathe. He is the air I breathe. It sounds so corny, it's so terrible. Half the time when I talk to him, I'll go, 'My God, what happened to me? I'm like a f***ing Hallmark card!' But…it's just a welcome relief to be able to just be settled. To actually know what home is."

Academy Awards (2001)

chapter 14

After Oscar

jolie confounded expectations following her Oscar win, not just with her marriage to Thornton but also with her next film. After the wearying shoots and dark subjects of both *The Bone Collector* and *Girl, Interrupted* (the latter of which Jolie, once again, found hard to disengage herself from), Jolie decided to lighten the mood with her role in *Gone in 60 Seconds*. "It's just a bunch of boys," Jolie said in an interview, "just what I needed. It was a script they gave me that was nothing but Ferraris, Nic Cage and Giovanni Ribisi and that sounded like a good idea. It's just a fun movie, and I tried to just have fun."

In a mark of her rising popularity and clout, Jolie was offered one of the three lead roles in Columbia's highly anticipated adaptation of the 1970s television series *Charlie's Angels*, but she refused (other actresses rumored to star in the film were Thandie Newton and Jada Pinkett-Smith), and her role eventually went to *Ally McBeal*'s Lucy Liu.

Some observers wondered why she would turn down *Charlie's Angels* (which, with its strong female and photogenic cast and hyperkinetic blend of comedy and action, opened in November 2000 to a whopping record-setting $40.3 million) and accept a much smaller part in *Gone in 60 Seconds*.

"The selling points of *Charlie's Angels* were the characters were strong women, and I've been able to do that," Jolie told *E!*. "Secondly, they said, 'It will make you a big star.' Which is frightening, and they said that was a plus...for me, it would've been just for money. I didn't really watch [the series] and

In a mark of her rising popularity and clout, Jolie was offered one of the three lead roles in Columbia's highly anticipated adaptation of the 1970s television series *Charlie's Angels*, but she refused...

I didn't find it fun. I don't get dressed up. For me, *Gone in 60 Seconds*—that's my fun movie." Jolie also expressed concerns that she just wouldn't fit in with her co-stars, Drew Barrymore and Cameron Diaz, because "they're celebrities in such a way that it's great they can make fun of themselves." She felt much more comfortable with the men, such as Nicolas Cage and Giovanni Ribisi of *Gone in 60 Seconds*.

A Jerry Bruckheimer production, *Gone in 60 Seconds* certainly wasn't going to be art-house fare, nor was it going to be long on characterization, depth or plot. Jerry Bruckheimer was the producer behind *Armageddon*, *Enemy of the State*, *Con Air* and *The Rock*. His films, though never critical favorites, were extremely popular with audiences, and he would eventually go on to marry critical and popular acclaim with his work in television on the top-ranked *CSI* franchise for CBS and the hugely popular *The Pirates of the Caribbean: The Curse of the Black Pearl*. This latter film has the double distinction of not only being based on an amusement park ride but also of securing Johnny Depp his first Academy Award nomination for Best Actor.

With *The Rock* and *Con Air*, Bruckheimer began a professional relationship with actor Nicolas Cage that continues to this day. Originally known for his quirky roles in *Moonstruck* and *Raising Arizona*, the famous nephew of director Francis Ford Coppola seemed destined to be denied any sort of mainstream success. Anytime Cage stepped out of the niche he had carved for himself, audiences and critics turned away. Flops, such as the *Top Gun* imitation *Fire Birds*, the romantic comedy *It Could Happen to You* and the failed David Caruso vehicle *Kiss of Death*, threatened to torpedo the goodwill and critical praises that Cage had won early in his career.

But then along came Mike Figgis' grim *Leaving Las Vegas*, the dark story of alcoholic Ben Sanderson (Cage), who arrives in Las Vegas with plans to drink himself to death. He finds redemption of sorts in the arms of Elisabeth Shue's Sera, a prostitute with whom he falls in love. The film was a critical success, earning Cage and Shue the best notices of their careers; Cage, Shue and Figgis all received Oscar nominations, and Cage collected a golden statuette as Best Actor.

Cage followed his win with successive turns in Bruckheimer productions, as fish-out-of-water Stanley Goodspeed in the relatively entertaining but ultimately noisy *The Rock* and as freed convict Cameron Poe in the preposterous *Con Air*. Both films were huge crowd-pleasing blockbusters, and though many questioned Cage's artistic decisions, the joy and off-kilter energy he brought to the films was undeniable.

> Cage's unlikely position as an action star was cemented in place in John Woo's praised and popular *Face/Off*, in which Cage and John Travolta gleefully and winningly chewed the scenery as an FBI agent and criminal genius who swap faces and identities.

Cage received another Oscar nomination for his work in the hilariously wry take on the writer's life in *Adaptation* and was praised for his role as a bested con man in *Matchstick Men*. He's an actor capable of winning over audiences and critics alike.

In *Gone in 60 Seconds*, Cage played Randall "Memphis" Raines, a retired car thief brought back into the game when, in order to save his brother's life, he must steal 50 luxury cars in just one night. Complicating matters are Delroy Lindos' Detective Roland Castlebeck, intent on bringing his nemesis Raines down, a rival crew planning the same heist and the return of ex-flame Sara "Sway" Wayland (Jolie, her dark hair replaced with blonde dreadlocks) to Randall's life.

> Jolie was trained in stunt driving by Bobby Ore and learned how to hot wire and steal a car...

The film is ostensibly a remake of the 1974 film of the same name, and it's not hard to see what drew Bruckheimer to the project. The 1974 film

is best remembered for a 40-minute extended car chase scene in which a total of 90 cars were destroyed. But save for the title and one clever scene, Bruckheimer's *Gone in 60 Seconds* bore little in common with its predecessor.

The cast of *Gone in 60 Seconds* featured a parade of faces familiar to Bruckheimer films, including Robert Duvall as sage Otto Halliwell (Duvall had played mentor to Tom Cruise in Bruckheimer's *Top Gun* on wheels, *Days of Thunder*) and Will Patton as friend Atley Jackson (he fulfilled a similar role as Bruce Willis' astronaut companion in *Armageddon*). There were new faces too, such as Giovanni Ribisi (cast as Randall's brother Kip), who had attracted audiences with his supporting roles on the sitcoms *The Wonder Years* and *Friends*, and British actor Christopher Eccleston (cast as villain Raymond Calitri), who had signaled his stateside arrival as the scheming and treacherous Duke of Norfolk in *Elizabeth*.

For the production, many of the actors in *Gone in 60 Seconds* were trained in stunt driving, with Cage adopting the research as a hobby after filming was completed. Jolie was trained in stunt driving by Bobby Ore and learned how to hot wire and steal a car, somewhat impractical skills, to be sure, but not without their satisfactions.

The film opened on June 9, 2000, and quickly outdid its competition. It knocked Tom Cruise's highly anticipated *MI:2* from its perch atop the box office with a weekend gross of $25.5 million. Additionally, it was undoubtedly the biggest opening for any film that Jolie had been associated with, but it was displaced (as has become common with summer films, which open large and fade quickly) the following week by Samuel L. Jackson's *Shaft*. In any event, *Gone in 60 Seconds* went on to gross over $100 million in the United States alone and more worldwide.

As expected, the film received middling reviews. Stephen Hunter of the *Washington Post* predictably punned the film's name in his critique, writing, "I'll tell you what's gone in 60 seconds, all right: my attention." Jay Carr of the *Boston Globe* called it "the flat tire of summer movies," and *Variety* deemed it "dreadful in every respect."

> Of course, it's easy to criticize summer audience-pleasers. These sorts of films are not made with critics in mind but with pocketbooks and an eye on return. Films like these are geared towards youth, the ones with disposable incomes and idle time during the summer break. In the end, these types of films are made to entertain, not to enlighten, and in its own way, **Gone in 60 Seconds** is a pleasing confection.

The plot and its complications notwithstanding (those tend to get tedious, and it's clear why three screenwriters took a stab at it), it's always fun watching pros go to work and do what they do best. It is in those moments, when Randall and his crew are fanning out across the city to steal the cars they've lovingly baptized Eleanor, Bernadene and Angelina (among others), that the film zips along at an enjoyable clip.

Jolie does what she can with a thinly written and ultimately thankless role, and she exudes a playful sexuality as Cage's mechanic car-thief and love interest. In the rare moments when she's onscreen, it's the wink and the gleam of mischief in her eye that inject the film with a burst of adrenaline, an energy otherwise lost beneath the Bruckheimer trademarks of machismo, alpha-male posturing and bright explosions.

Gone in 60 Seconds left many people wondering what Jolie was doing to her reputation, one built upon her dramatic roles in *Gia* and *Girl, Interrupted*, but the actress refused to take herself too seriously. "I want to play a character, I want to go crazy, and I want to play with cars," Jolie said in an interview with the World Entertainment News Network. "If that means I don't have an image of a 'serious actress,' then fine." In fact, *Gone in 60 Seconds* was only a prelude to what would be Jolie's most successful and, arguably, most commercial project, *Lara Croft: Tomb Raider*, in which she would don the tank tops and guns that she had dismissed as a teenager fresh from her role in *Hackers*.

chapter 15

lara
Croft

n 1996, video game publisher Eidos unveiled its latest offering, Tomb Raider, designed by Core Design Limited. Core Design, which had scored minor successes with titles such as Rick Dangerous, could not have anticipated how quickly its heroine, British archaeologist Lara Croft, would become one of the most iconic and prolific characters in video game history: the sexy and empowered face of the digital age. In short order, Tomb Raider was largely responsible for Sony's dominance in the gaming console industry—thousands of people bought its PlayStation specifically to play Tomb Raider. Lara Croft appeared in the newspapers of *The Financial Times* and *The Sunday Telegraph* and on magazine covers such as *FACE*. In addition, clothing companies, such as the outdoor apparel giant Timberland, approached Core Design with endorsement deals. Indeed, in the inevitable video game sequel, Lara Croft became a fashion model of sorts, appearing in the apparel of swimsuit company Sola.

Although the game itself is a fluid, intelligent and highly satisfying adventure, among the best in the genre, most of Tomb Raider's success can be attributed to its buxom heroine. Adventure games of the time rarely strayed from the tough-guy heroes who had been a staple of video games since their inception. A heroine, not just attractive but also intelligent, courageous and agile, was nothing short of revolutionary. Lara Croft, a female Indiana Jones, had an appeal that spanned the sexes: boys could ogle the pixilated archaeologist, while girls finally had a great female character they could call their own. Over time, five Tomb Raider sequels were released and, all

combined, they have sold over 30 million copies. Its success did not go unnoticed.

Offers to adapt the video game to film poured into Core Design's offices just after the launch of Tomb Raider II. Core Design approached the opportunities with trepidation and a sense of dread. After all, the filmic adaptations of the popular video games of Streetfighter, Double Dragon, Mortal Kombat and Super Mario Brothers had been spectacular failures. They were crippled by plots and concepts that proved pitifully and simply lame. One proposal, however, did catch Core Design's eye. It came from Paramount Pictures and from producer Lawrence Gordon (who had produced the 1980s staples *Die Hard* and *Predator*) and his business partner Lloyd Levin (who had produced *Boogie Nights*).

Levin was a fan of the game and said in an interview that he and Gordon "pursued the movie rights because it had a real character at its center, and the game's storylines were very cinematic in approach....Tomb Raider offered something that hadn't been seen in movies before: exotic adventure, thrilling action, treasure hunts and mortal danger, all given a very modern spin with a unique character...embodying the spirit of contemporary cool."

In their pitch to Core Design, Gordon and Levin promised that they would work slowly and would be extremely careful not to disrupt the game's meticulously crafted mythology. Core Design was sold on their idea and, in 1997, Gordon and Levin acquired the rights to the film. Scripts were ushered into development but few managed to capture the flavor or personality of the game itself, and for a long while, it looked as if the picture might languish forever in development hell. A director and 11 separate writers came and went.

The picture didn't come together until December 1999, when Simon West (highly profitable director of the Bruckheimer noisy extravaganza *Con Air* and *The General's Daughter*), who had turned the project down twice, finally decided to accept. However, West was unhappy with the latest script and decided to begin anew, finding inspiration in the epics *Dr. Zhivago* and *Lawrence of Arabia*. He delved into research on mysticism, sacred geometry, religious rites and astrology and delivered a completed screenplay in May 2000.

In West's story, a secret society known as the Illuminati is on a quest to find an ancient clock that is capable of opening up both space and time. The clock, however, is only the beginning. It is, essentially, a map of sorts that will lead to the two halves of a mystical triangle that, when combined, can stop time. The Illuminati are determined to use the device to resurrect their forebears and alter the fate of mankind. The only hitch to their plan for global domination? The clock is in the hands of archaeologist Lara Croft, and she means to keep it from the Illuminati and save the world.

With a director, a script and a reported $80 million budget, all West needed now was a star. For months, the media watched and waited to hear who would be cast as the iconic heroine. Whoever received the role would surely reach heights of superstardom; the film, with its rare, strong female lead, was virtually a guaranteed blockbuster. Legions of fans were salivating to see Lara Croft in the flesh. The film also promised to be the start of a lucrative

...for a long while, it looked as if the picture might languish forever in development hell. A director and 11 separate writers came and went.

Lara Croft: Tomb Raider (2001)

franchise along the lines of Warner Brothers' *Batman* (which ultimately flamed out in its fourth, painful installment, *Batman & Robin*) and Paramount's own highly lucrative *Mission: Impossible*.

> Studios are notoriously fond of franchises, and it's not hard to see why. Sequels typically outdo their predecessors at the box office and establish a built-in audience eager to see familiar characters. The potential financial rewards, not only for the studio but also for the star, are potent lures.

Numerous names were bandied about in the press as speculation about Lara Croft's casting intensified. Would she be played by Sandra Bullock, a hot property since *Speed* had made her a household name? Or would it resurrect the career of Demi Moore? Or would it be recent Bond babe Denise Richards? Or British actress and model Elizabeth Hurley? Or Catherine Zeta-Jones? Or Jennifer Love-Hewitt? West, for his part, maintained in an online interview that the only actress he ever had in mind was Angelina Jolie. "It was a one-horse race," he said. "If she didn't do it, I couldn't think of anyone else. All of her performances have been a heady combination of gorgeously voluptuous womanhood but with brains, wit and good humor. Those were the attributes Lara had to have, and Angelina embodied them…I also instinctively knew she would satisfy the demands of the game's fans and their preconceived ideas of what Lara looked like."

Jolie accepted the role—tank tops, guns and all—because she was intrigued by the novelty of doing what she called a "blockbuster fantasy." The role also represented, to a degree, a character quite unlike anything Jolie had embodied before. "It's much easier to internalize and remain dark," Jolie said in an interview with Preview Online, alluding to her Oscar-winning turn in *Girl, Interrupted*, "which is what I've been used to playing up until now. [Playing Lara Croft] was the hardest job I've ever done: she's very clear about herself and her goals and overly capable in an almost beyond-human way. It's hard to stay in a positive, healthy, clear and brave state of mind all the time."

Although the role was challenging, Jolie also found that the essence of Lara Croft was, in some ways, similar to many of her previous outings. "She's alone, focused on justice, is a little crazy in many ways, bold, loves her freedom and is very sexual," she elaborated. "Those are traits I adore in people in general and themes I've explored in movies before."

And though still married to Thornton, Jolie spent much of the shoot away from her husband. Thornton, who is known to be afraid of flying, was unwilling to brave the 11-hour transatlantic flight. The demanding shooting schedule gave Jolie little time off, and the couple continued their relationship much as it had began: over the phone. Jolie lamented, "I'm on the phone to him every night crying like a baby and saying, 'I miss you.' I love him so much." It was easy to lose herself in the work, however. For the 20-week shoot, Jolie appeared in nearly every scene. And then, of course, there were the stunts.

Insisting that she do her own stunts, Jolie was required to make lifestyle and diet changes. The cigarettes, caffeine, sugar and alcohol were replaced with water, vitamins and a grueling work-out regimen (although Jolie would say, as is her wont, that "having sex with my husband keeps me in much more shape"). Taxing as her three-month physical training was, Jolie was adamant. "We realized early on that because of the type of character she was, you can't pretend to be her," she said. "You have to be her. You can't pretend to do the stunts and wear the guns and shoot them, run around and live in that house. She actually does those things." There were times when Jolie, bruised and battered, returned to her home, sat in the tub and cried, worried that Paramount might have made a mistake in casting her.

Jolie truly did suffer for her art. She injured her knee when she fell off a climbing wall,

> Jolie accepted the role—tank tops, guns and all—because she was intrigued by the novelty of doing what she called a "blockbuster fantasy."

tore ligaments in her foot while jumping, aggravated her shoulder after months of boxing and, during the film's bungee ballet sequence, bled from doing triple somersaults and climbing, with a wire, up and down walls. At one point, Jolie told *Premiere* that she thought that she was developing abdominal muscles "but they were actually big bruises that were puffing up." In the end, however, it was the skimpy shorts that Jolie had the biggest problems with. "I don't ever wear miniskirts or shorts," she told *Premiere*. "And all day long, I was pulling them down or keeping my legs crossed. After a while, it was kind of fun to feel sexual and provocative."

> Wardrobe issues aside, all who worked on the troubled shoot agreed that Jolie was the least of their concerns. "I'd put Angelina under a lifetime contract if I could," producer Gordon raved to **Premiere**. "She may be the only thing we didn't have a problem with on this movie."

The film was shot over five months, beginning in London's Pinewood Studios before decamping for locations as exotic and varied as Hofn, Iceland and the 12th-century temples of Angkor Wat in Cambodia. Its international cast featured Iain Glen of *Gorillas in the Mist*, Noah Taylor of *Shine* (in the role that had been reportedly offered to Jolie's ex-husband, Jonny Lee Miller), Daniel Craig of *Elizabeth* and, marking the first collaboration with his daughter since *Lookin' to Get Out*, Jon Voight.

Voight was cast as Lara Croft's late archaeologist father, Lord Richard Croft. Father and daughter shared only one scene together, undoubtedly the emotional climax of the film in which Lara, traveling through time, tenderly and tearfully reconciles with her father. There was no question that the scene resonated deeply with both Voight and Jolie, who shared their own fractious and divided past. "The story had to do with her connecting to her father," Jolie told *Premiere*. "So we decided the scene would be about us really speaking to each other."

In an online interview, Voight said, "Angie and I have talked about working together before, but neither of us saw the *Tomb Raider* opportunity until the last minute. I didn't want to rain on her star parade and have our professional relationship interfering with our tight family one." The project brought the two closer together, and watching his daughter act was something else. "Watching her perform up close, I could see the emotional risks she was taking," Voight said. "I'm extremely proud, and we're very close and so we're very happy these days. It's a very beautiful time for us."

With shooting on the film wrapped, *Lara Croft: Tomb Raider* was slated for release on June 15, 2001, and for the first time, Jolie was front and center, carrying a film on her shoulders alone. If the film was a success, it would surely signal the arrival of not just an actress but a profitable one too. If not, then it would be a spectacular failure and one that would most certainly dispel much of the attendant goodwill and support of her Oscar win. Anxieties ran high, as did expectations.

Lara Croft: Tomb Raider turned out to be a spectacular mess. Its roots in the *Indiana Jones* trilogy are obvious, but by no means is the film as enjoyable. The locations are certainly stunning, as are the outfits that Lara Croft wears throughout her journeys, but besides the eye candy, there is little nourishing here. For all the manic pacing and editing, the film still feels sluggish, mired as it is in its own inflated sense of importance. The plot itself is confusing and convoluted, as if it had been conceived solely to

117

enable the director and crew to travel to its exotic locations (which every adventure film must have).

There are faint glimmers of excitement contained within the numerous action pieces, but these scenes have been edited and cut to the point that they become just a visual mishmash of images that rarely allow for the audience to sit back and exhale with wonder. As it is in so many of her films, Jolie is the best thing about *Lara Croft: Tomb Raider*. She speaks in clipped tones with a more than adequate posh British accent, bears an uncanny physical resemblance to the digital heroine, and she almost manages to rescue the script with her winking smirks, charisma and cockiness.

Unfortunately, Jolie was saddled with a character written with little depth; she is, in the end, playing just a character from a video game: flat and two-dimensional. Lost for what to do with

Lara Croft Tomb Raider: Cradle of Life (2003)

their heroine, the writers seemed content to flesh her out by satisfying every boy's fantasy. There's a shot here of Lara showering and a lingering and extended shot there of Lara running with her heaving, pneumatic breasts. The villains are mere caricatures. All that is missing from Iain Glen's Manfred Powell is a long, thin mustache to twirl while cackling maniacally. Playing Lara's ambiguous love interest Alex West, Daniel Craig often seems lost but it's not his fault. His character feels tacked on, his presence isn't crucial to either the plot or character development, and he really isn't given all that much to do. The plot, such as it is, is an incoherent jumble that only reminds people of how poor a job the film did in aping *Raiders of the Lost Ark*.

Mick LaSalle, writing for the *San Francisco Chronicle*, opined that "there are a few good moments that prevent *Tomb Raider* from being one of the worst films of the year. But they're not enough to make it worth seeing." Talk about damning with faint praise. *Newsweek*'s Brian Giles wrote that *Lara Croft: Tomb Raider* "couldn't have arrived at a better time: movies have been so bad lately that audiences are positively starving for something mediocre." Kenneth Turan of the *Los Angeles Times* wrote that the movie is "almost completely lacking in genuine thrills. Even the attractive presence of star Angelina Jolie can't keep this leaden, plodding, completely underwhelming film from playing like 'Lara Croft: Yawn Inducer.'"

Lara Croft: Tomb Raider overcame the scathing reviews in its opening weekend by topping the box office with $47.7 million. It set a record, of sorts, for the biggest opening for a film based on a video game (the previous record holder was *Poké-mon: The First Movie*, which opened with $31 million) and quickly swept away any lingering bad tastes left over from the releases of *Streetfighter* and its ilk. The following week,

> As it is in so many of her films, Jolie is the best thing about *Lara Croft: Tomb Raider*.

Lara Croft Tomb Raider: Cradle of Life (2003)

the cumulative effect of poor reviews and bad word of mouth took their toll (at test screenings, audiences reportedly chatted throughout the movie, laughed at inappropriate times and left the theaters shaking their heads and muttering), and *Lara Croft: Tomb Raider* tumbled from first to third in just a week, taking in $19.8 million, which was a 59% drop-off from the week before, bested by *The Fast and the Furious* and *Dr. Dolittle 2*. Still, the film went on to gross over $130 million domestically and even more overseas, guaranteeing that there would indeed be a sequel and securing the franchise Paramount had been seeking, terrible reviews aside.

> Jolie signed on to do two sequels, admitting that while she had initially disliked Lara Croft, she had now come to see her as a "weird little friend." With the success of **Lara Croft: Tomb Raider**, Jolie was now a bona fide superstar, and her marriage to Billy Bob Thornton assured her of a place in the tabloids.

But something had happened to the actress during the filming of *Lara Croft: Tomb Raider*. A transformation was afoot, and it would lead Jolie to her most prominent role, one rarely discussed in the media with the same scrutiny and doggedness as her private life and public life as an actress. This transformation would help Jolie discover the joys of motherhood, but it would also lead to the eventual dissolution of her marriage to Billy Bob Thornton.

chapter 16

The Ambassador

Returning from Cambodia in 2001 after the filming of *Lara Croft: Tomb Raider*, Jolie arrived at the Beverly Hills home she shared with her husband. Thornton was downstairs in his recording studio, attending to his other passion in life: music. He was working on his debut album (which would eventually be released to great derision and mockery). While alone in the upstairs bedroom of their palatial home, a home located in a state with the fifth-largest economy in the world, Jolie's mind was unable to bridge the disconnect between her life here and the lives of those in Cambodia. Cambodia was a war-ravaged country that had been blown back into the stone age by the Khmer Rouge and had yet to recover from that dark chapter in its history. Jolie felt an overwhelming sense of shame.

"I thought I knew what suffering was," she told *GQ* in March 2004. "I had no idea what suffering was. I had never seen real poverty. And I had never met people like that. People who had been through war, genocide, occupation. People whose children had had their legs blown off 30 years after the war had ended by land mines that had been waiting for them in the soil—but who still had humor and grace. I was angry and ashamed by what I didn't know. It's not that I suddenly wanted to 'help.' More that I had a sudden need to find out what else I didn't know."

Jolie was angry, unable to understand how her country, a nation of such fortune and opportunity, could be so ignorant to the suffering of millions. It was a reality she had

> "I thought I knew what suffering was," she told **GQ** in March 2004. "I had no idea what suffering was."

never seen in the history texts of her education. She began to read, poring over books and atlases, United Nations reports and maps, girding herself with an education in the devastation of Southeast Asia, of Pol Pot and Cambodia, Vietnam and Laos.

"While I was doing this, Billy was downstairs recording his album," Jolie continued to *GQ*. "Something about that registered. I actually thought, 'This will be the moment that our marriage divides.' Looking back, that was absolutely the evening it did. For people who spend months and months apart doing films, it is possible to wake up one day and realize, you've changed."

> Hollywood celebrities are often lampooned for their commitment to social causes and are dismissed as being self-righteous, while the more cynical view their sympathies, good intentions aside, as thinly veiled attempts to gain humanitarian credibility. After all, when you're making millions, living a fabulously spoiled life of perks and wealth, it's easy to become a champion of causes. But at the same time, there's a whiff of self-serving hypocrisy about it all.

There are those, however, who are undeniably committed to their causes, investing not just lip service but also their time and money to enlighten themselves, to educate and to learn. They use their positions as celebrities, with its accompanying influence and power, to effect some societal good. And if no one seems to notice or to care, it makes little difference to them. So it was with Jolie. While everyone was discussing the upcoming *Lara Croft: Tomb Raider* and exchanging the latest gossip about Angelina and Billy Bob, Jolie was living and breathing her research.

Drawn to the plight of refugees, Jolie began making phone calls and was referred to the United Nations High Commission on Refugees (UNHCR), a sister agency of the United Nations (UN). In the call, she said, according to an interview she gave on National Public Radio (NPR), "You might think I'm crazy. I'm an actress. I don't want to go with press. If you could give me access, allow me in on a trip so I could just witness and learn." The agency, no doubt realizing what an opportunity they had to publicize their cause, invited Jolie to Washington. She told her husband she was going, to which Thornton responded, "Okay. Good luck. Bye. Have a nice trip." The trip to Washington led to a two-week journey through Sierra Leone, ravaged and still convulsing from the civil war fought between the government and the Revolutionary United Front. Thornton did not share Jolie's excitement about the trip, but he did fear for her safety. She asked him to come but he refused.

> "He didn't want me to go through that door," she recalled. "He said he didn't think I'd be safe. But he didn't offer to come along, either. And so I left. And when I came back two weeks later, I was a very different person."

Visits to Tanzania, Pakistan, Cote D'Ivoire and Cambodia followed, during which Jolie kept a journal and which she subsequently posted on the Internet to publicize the work of the UNHCR. Her work, done without press, and at her own expense, clearly illustrated Jolie's commitment. "You don't understand how it happened," Jolie said to NPR, "you can't understand how nobody told you. Somehow it wasn't important enough or somebody decided that you shouldn't."

On August 27, 2001, Jolie became the Goodwill Ambassador for the UNHCR (positions once held by both Richard Burton and Sophia Loren). She was determined to rectify the situation. High Commissioner Ruud Lubbers said at the time that he hoped Jolie would "convince a younger generation that something has to be done." To that end, Jolie testified before Congress on the

plight of refugees and donated millions of dollars to help Afghan refugees, to establish a Cambodia wildlife preserve, to rebuild a hospital in Sri Lanka and to establish educational programs for the many refugees amassed along the Thai-Myanmar border. In her role as Goodwill Ambassador, Jolie continued to travel, visiting refugee camps located in the notorious danger zones of the Balkans, Namibia, Congo, Jordan, Colombia and Ecuador. Her passion and zeal for the work won the praises of UN officials, who called her dedication "exceptional."

A year later, on August 23, 2002, Jolie received another award to go along with her Oscar; she became the first recipient of the Church World Service Immigration and Refugee Program Humanitarian Award. At the ceremony, Jolie was praised for her work and called "a role model of individual humanitarian action, an inspiration to people around the world, especially the young. She gives a voice to the often forgotten refugees and displaced persons whose lives have been torn apart by persecution and war. Her active concern brings the promise of hope."

It was a transformation few could believe. After all, just years before, Jolie had been the teenager contemplating

> "You might think I'm crazy. I'm an actress. I don't want to go with press. If you could give me access, allow me in on a trip so I could just witness and learn."

suicide and unable to grasp a world beyond that mapped out through her own misery. The younger Jolie did tend to flagellate towards self-indulgence, but really, what young adult doesn't? Jolie entered the limelight somewhat unformed (she was only 19, after all), still without a clear idea of who she was or what she was. That she could, with such apparent ease and devotion, transform herself into a literate, plainspoken and humble advocate for the rights of Third World refugees is nothing less than a further definition and expansion of who Jolie is. She is a passionate and zealous actress; she is also a passionate and zealous advocate.

> What's rendered most clearly is that Jolie, media portrayals to the contrary, is a serious woman, an individual who approaches everything she does with professionalism. What is shocking is the shock itself. Society has come to expect so little from its celebrities (think Jennifer Lopez and others of her ilk warbling away on albums that bemoan the pitfalls and perils of their fame while celebrating their own luxurious selves) that when one comes along and transcends expectations, people react almost negatively, with disbelief and, in some circles, derision.

Jolie has a reputation in the film industry for being an anti-diva: a populist actress who shows up promptly, eschews the perks and never divides herself from the crew. It's the same sort of workman-like mentality she brings to her work as a Goodwill Ambassador. She rarely trumpets her advocacy work in the press, speaking only when and where needed, such as in March 2004 when she called on the world to help the UNCHR raise the

$20 million it deemed necessary to help Sudanese refugees in Chad. At the same time, she donated $50,000 to water projects in that African country to help the thousands of Sudanese refugees displaced from war-torn Darfur.

According to a UN spokesman, Jolie was the first person to make a major, private donation to the UNCHR's emergency appeal for Chad. Even the publishing of her journals in late 2003, *Notes from My Travels: Visits with Refugees in Africa, Cambodia, Pakistan and Ecuador,* was released with little fanfare, and her writing, elegant, subtle and sparse, is effectively persuasive and moving.

The travels proved therapeutic for Jolie. In an interview with *Us Weekly* Jolie said, "Anyone who's identified with me by feeling alone or a bit crazy should know I've figured it out. Get outside yourself. Get outside your environment. Do something for other people." In *Vogue,* she elaborated. "It's done more for me than I think I could ever do for them," she said. "Though I hope to do more for them."

chapter 17

Maddox

When Jolie returned to Cambodia in November 2001, this time accompanied by Thornton, she toured an orphanage. While there, the couple came upon a little boy with whom they felt an immediate connection, and they began the process of adopting him. It was a lengthy process, full of detailed background checks and bureaucratic red tape.

The process was further complicated when Jolie's father announced at an Academy Awards luncheon in March 2002 that he was a grandfather. Voight's gaffe caught the attention of the United States government, which had banned the adoption of Cambodian babies the year before. Jolie and Thornton's case was investigated and finally dismissed, delaying the child's American visa. Voight's revelation caught the couple by surprise; after all, they had wanted to make the announcement themselves. Indeed, Jolie had no idea that her father was even aware of her plans. The two had hardly spoken since filming on *Lara Croft: Tomb Raider* had wrapped. Although Lara and her father had parted on good terms, this was not the case for Jolie and her father.

"After *Tomb Raider*, he said some very ugly things to me about what he thought I was like as a person and how I was conducting my life," she told *GQ*. "At first, I was completely surprised and injured by it. But then, things became clear: This is a person who for the most part has either been absent from my life or been creating a lot of ugliness in it. I don't have to have him in my life. For myself, for my son, I need to be healthy—I don't need drama. I don't want him around." Despite Voight's assertions to the contrary (he had, after all, said earlier that after *Tomb Raider* he and his daughter were never happier), Jolie had had enough of her father.

Voight's meddling, along with the announcement in early 2002 that he was a grandfather, puzzled and confused many observers. Most famous of all, Voight began a string of bizarre appearances on news programs like *Access Hollywood* and *Inside Edition* in which he tearfully pleaded for his daughter to seek psychiatric help, saying that she had "serious mental problems." It had been his hope that his daughter would see the interviews and call him. She didn't.

Ironically, Jolie had long ago sought out a psychiatrist to help with her familial issues but dismissed the help when the therapist seemed a little too happy to hear about a morbid dream in which Jolie had attacked and stabbed her father with a fork. Jolie was incensed by her father's claims and understandably concerned that they might very well scotch her adoption plans. She excised him from her life and, in one final act, officially dropped her father's name at a court in Santa Monica later that year.

Despite Voight's pleas for reconciliation, Jolie remains steadfastly unmoved, unwilling, it's been said, to subject her son to her father's brand of fickle love. For his part, Voight genuinely appears to fear for his daughter's mental well-being, but his good intentions have done little to restore their relationship.

Putting her concerns aside, in May 2002 Jolie and Thornton became the proud parents of Maddox Chivan Thornton Jolie. Maddox joined Jolie in Africa, where she was filming *Beyond Borders* (a troubled production which, eerily enough, recounted the spiritual awakening of a spoiled American woman who is spurred to crusade for the rights of Third World refugees), and in early June, the family was reunited in the United States. The family appeared

> Jolie was incensed by her father's claims and understandably concerned that they might very well scotch her adoption plans.

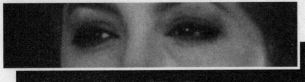

JOLIE FAN FACT

When Angelina began building her home in Cambodia (to bring her son closer to his homeland), she ran into some complications. The land had to be de-mined.

happy enough at the time, though Maddox's arrival might have been the catalyst for the couple's eventual divorce.

Thornton, already the father of three children from previous marriages, resumed touring in support of his rock album, *Private Radio*, and rumors grew about his alleged infidelities. *USA Weekly* reported that while in Columbus, Ohio, Thornton, his assistant and a bandmate arrived at a restaurant where, for privacy, they were offered the VIP room. Thornton refused, choosing instead to sit with a group of twenty-something women. One of the women allegedly asked whether Thornton truly did wear a vial of his wife's blood around his neck, and Thornton is said to have responded, "That's just a myth."

Those close to Thornton denied the rumors, but to friends and family, it was clear that the marriage was headed towards divorce. The pair had moved out of their Beverly Hills home, and Jolie and Maddox were living in a small hotel mere miles away. In June 2002, Jolie filed for divorce, citing irreconcilable differences. Jolie was devastated.

"I'm angry. I'm sad. It's a very difficult and sad time," she said in an interview. "Sometimes you don't see things coming, even though they are happening. It's not that simple to say this or that one thing caused the problems, but it's clear to me that our priorities shifted overnight. He's focused on his music and career, and I'm focused on my baby. It comes down to what's important to you. Good for him. But I have other priorities."

Taking Maddox with her, Jolie went on trips to Thailand and found solace in her family. She told *USA Weekly,* "I have a good family—my mother and brother and the people I'm working with. I am surrounded by good people." Few could help but notice that she neglected to mention her father.

> The separation from Thornton left Jolie angry, but she spent a great deal of her time controlling it for the sake of her son. "He gets sad when I'm sad," she said. "I really want to stay in a good space for my kid."

Jolie banished all reminders of Thornton from her life, including the painful removal of a host of tattoos that proclaimed her undying affection for the erstwhile musician. The divorce was finalized in early 2003, and Jolie was (to the great delight of her male and some female fans) officially single again. Life for Jolie, it seems, has always been either one of successive fortunes or successive tragedies. Just as her private life spiraled away from her, her film career similarly foundered.

chapter 18

After Lara and Beyond

Lara Croft: Tomb Raider had surpassed expectations and placed Jolie among the ranks of leading ladies such as Julia Roberts and Cameron Diaz. But the films that followed the blockbuster all proved underwhelming, and Jolie's acting career entered the sort of tailspin that can spell disaster. In the wake of these failures, carping could be heard that her greatest commercial success had less to do with Jolie than with a built-in audience long clamoring for a Tomb Raider film. Hopes had been high for the next films that Jolie played in: the steamy thriller Original Sin, Jolie's first purely comedic role in Life or Something Like It and the drama Beyond Borders that boasted actor of the moment Clive Owen as Jolie's romantic foil.

Original Sin, an adaptation of Cornell Woolrich's novel Waltz into Darkness, opened to tepid reviews—deemed a "bad apple" by USA Today's Mike Clark, "forgettable" by The New York Times' Elvis Mitchell and "run-of-the-mill trash" by the San Francisco Chronicle's Wesley Morris. Audiences found little appealing about the film as well, and it was quickly forgotten.

Life or Something Like It, in which Jolie starred with Ed Burns (squandering the credibility he had amassed with The Brothers McMullen and Saving Private Ryan) as a television reporter whose seemingly perfect life is disrupted with the prophecies of a soothsaying homeless man (he predicts that she will die within a week), was meant to be a light romantic comedy. It is, however, such a

Lara Croft: Tomb Raider had surpassed expectations and placed Jolie among the ranks of leading ladies such as Julia Roberts and Cameron Diaz.

Life or Something Like It (2002)

heavy load of saccharine sentiments that it never manages to rise above its clichés and most unfortunate of all, never surprises.

Beyond Borders, a film that surely must have held a place close to Jolie's heart, was troubled from the start. Oliver Stone had originally intended to direct the love story but begged off to turn his attentions to his biopic, **Alexander**. Kevin Costner had been cast as the lead but he departed citing creative differences. Clive Owen, much buzzed about thanks to his roles in **Croupier** and **Gosford Park**, then stepped in.

The film's story, detailing the romance between an international relief worker and an ignorant and sheltered philanthropist socialite, may have had more than a few similarities between fact and fiction. It also may have tackled subject matter usually swept under our collective rugs, but it is,

Life or Something Like It (2002)

finally, a sanctimonious film that is, as the *Wall Street Journal*'s Joe Morgenstern points out, "a sudsless soap opera with human misery as a backdrop for romantic banality." Critics called Jolie's performance "implausible." Owen Glieberman, of *Entertainment Weekly*, who had long been one of Jolie's staunchest supporters, laments that "Jolie, in this movie at least, has exactly two expressions: blank wistfulness and blank dismay."

Although this succession of bombs might have been enough to destroy any actor's career, Jolie has, perhaps not so surprisingly, remained relatively impervious. Even the colossal failure of *Lara Croft Tomb Raider: The Cradle of Life*, which received scathing reviews and failed to surpass or even approach the success of the original (and which essentially doomed plans for the no longer profitable franchise), has appeared to do little damage to Jolie's career. She is still among the highest paid actresses and, in 2004, her face could be seen everywhere, gracing the covers of magazines of *Entertainment Weekly*, *Esquire* (which called her The Sexiest Woman Alive), *GQ*, *Premiere* and others.

Wisely, Jolie chose to scale back on her starring roles; instead, she accepted minor supporting roles that maintained yet reduced her visibility. She was the voice of Lola in DreamWorks' *Shark Tale*, a film that was another attempt to ape the phenomenal critical and popular success of Pixar releases such as *Finding Nemo*, *Monsters, Inc.* and *Toy Story*. She also appeared in what basically amounted to a cameo role as an eye-patch-wearing pilot ace in Kerry Conran's visually opulent and stunning *Sky Captain and the World of Tomorrow.*

There was also the disappointing opening of Oliver Stone's labor of love, ***Alexander***, in which Jolie appears as Olympias, mother to Colin Farrell's Alexander and husband to Val Kilmer's Philip. The film, with a reported $150 million budget, had been in the back of Stone's mind for 15 years. Undoubtedly one of the most anticipated films of 2004 (Stone, the provocative director of ***Platoon***, ***JFK*** and ***Any Given Sunday,*** hadn't released a feature film since 1999), ***Alexander*** opened dismally and was more notable for the rumors circulating during that time, which had Jolie bedding almost every one of her male co-stars.

Indeed, after a year and a half of celibacy following her divorce, Jolie declared that she "had taken a lover," and curiosity as to who it might be ran rampant. Jolie has been linked to Ethan Hawke, her co-star in *Taking Lives,* and most spectacularly, to *Mr. and Mrs. Smith*'s Brad Pitt, who allegedly longs to start a family with his seemingly reluctant wife, Jennifer Aniston. Jolie, of course, has long expressed a desire to adopt more children, to build herself a "rainbow family," and if the tabloids are to be believed, it is apparently this mutual desire for children that has formed the basis for Pitt's and Jolie's union.

Most recently, Jolie has visited Russian orphanages, amidst sinister whispers from the tabloid *Daily Mail* that Jolie adopted a boy, not from an orphanage but had somehow "acquired" the

Sky Captain and the World of Tomorrow (2004)

child from an impoverished Russian woman. Even if the allegations are unfounded, Russian politicians have lambasted Jolie's adoption attempts, citing that she has circumvented official regulations. Indeed, these charges came just a few weeks after the revelation that the Hawaiian woman who had helped Jolie adopt Maddox had pleaded guilty to fraud and money laundering. Most damning of all, the agent, Lauryn Galindo, admitted paying as little as $100 to impoverished parents for their children, who Galindo then passed off as orphans while charging as much as $10,000 from Americans eager to adopt.

It's unclear how Jolie's acting career will be affected by the failure of *Alexander* and the scandals surrounding the adoption. Observers will be watching the high-concept *Mr. and Mrs. Smith* closely. With Pitt co-starring and proven director Doug Liman (*Go* and *The Bourne Identity*) at the helm, *Mr. and Mrs. Smith* has vast potential. However, one suspects that Jolie will emerge relatively unscathed; she has been remarkably buoyant in the past, blessed with an appeal that never seems to dim.

Alexander (2004)

Simply, Jolie is more than an actress. She is a personality, a star whose transparency has endeared her to fans and whose fame only appears to grow with each relative flop. Hers is a charisma that marries both glamour and accessibility, a decency that feels rare and must therefore be cherished.

> In the end, Jolie is likely grateful for the advice Marcheline Bertrand once bequeathed to her young daughter: be brave, be bold, be free. It is truly a maxim that Jolie has taken to heart.

If fans worry that Jolie's personality might be tempered with the domesticity of motherhood, they should take heart. Although Jolie has not been as open as she was in the past, she has cryptically referred to a life far more hedonistic and wild than the tabloids ever reported, leaving no doubt that Jolie will always be, as she put it so succinctly and precisely, an "evil queen."

Love and Honor (2006)

The Good Shepherd (2006)

Mr. and Mrs. Smith (2005)

Alexander (2004)

Sky Captain and the World of Tomorrow (2004)

Shark Tale (2004)

Taking Lives (2004)

Beyond Borders (2003)

Lara Croft Tomb Raider: The Cradle of Life (2003)

Life or Something Like It (2002)

Original Sin (2001)

Lara Croft: Tomb Raider (2001)

Gone in 60 Seconds (2000)

Girl, Interrupted (1999)

The Bone Collector (1999)

Pushing Tin (1999)

Playing by Heart (1998)

Hell's Kitchen (1998)

Gia (1998) (TV)

Playing God (1997)

George Wallace (1997) (TV)

True Women (1997) (TV)

Mojave Moon (1996)

Foxfire (1996)

Love Is All There Is (1996)

Without Evidence (1995)

Hackers (1995)

Bat Out of Hell II: Picture Show (1994)

Alice & Vini (1993)

Cyborg 2: Glass Shadow (1993)

Lookin' to Get Out (1982)

Notes on Sources

B, June 2001.

Internet Movie Database, http://www.imdb.com/.

Empire, June 1996, July 2001.

GQ, March 2004.

Premiere, October 1999, December 2000.

Rolling Stone, August 1999, July 2001, July 2003.

Vogue, April 2002.